ENDGAME

Rónán McDonald is a director of The Beckett International
Foundation and Senior Lecturer in English at the University
of Reading. He is the author of *Tragedy and Irish Literature:
Synge, O'Casey and Beckett* (2002), the *Cambridge Introduction
to Samuel Beckett* (2006) and *The Death of the Critic* (2007).

SAMUEL BECKETT

Endgame

Preface by Rónán McDonald

faber and faber

First published in 1958
by Faber and Faber Ltd
Bloomsbury House
74–77 Great Russell Street
London WC1B 3DA

Paperback edition first published in 1964
Reset in 2006
This edition first published in 2009

Typeset byRefineCatch Limited, Bungay, Suffolk
Printed and bound by CPI Group (UK) Ltd, Croydon, CR0 4YY

All applications for performing rights should be addressed to:
Curtis Brown Ltd, 4th Floor, Haymarket House,
28/29 Haymarket, London SW1 4SP

The right of Samuel Beckett to be identified as author of this work
has been asserted in accordance with Section 77 of the Copyright,
Designs and Patents Act 1988

The right of Rónán McDonald to be identified as editor of this work
has been asserted in accordance with Section 77 of the Copyright,
Designs and Patents Act 1988

A CIP record for this book
is available from the British Library

ISBN 978-0-571-24373-0

6 8 10 9 7

Contents

Preface

I

Endgame was originally written in French, as *Fin de partie* (1957), and subsequently translated into English by Beckett himself. While *En attendant Godot*, which brought Beckett fame in 1953, flowed as a distraction from the more taxing business (as he saw it) of prose composition, its successor was born slowly and painfully. *Waiting for Godot* had created a revolution in theatre, forcing leading critics like Kenneth Tynan to 're-examine the rules which have hitherto governed the drama; and, having done so, to pronounce them not elastic enough'.[1] How to follow up such a play? Beckett never repeated himself and never yielded to the appetite for reassuringly familiar forms and styles. Yet the need to find a new dramatic idiom proved testing. Especially so at a time when, after his great post-war creative flourishing (that included *Waiting for Godot*, *Endgame* and his trilogy of novels, *Molloy*, *Malone Dies*, *The Unnamable*), Beckett found himself in a creative impasse.

There are dramatic situations resembling *Fin de partie* in Beckett's notebooks from as early as 1950, but he began substantial work on the play in late 1954 and early 1955. During this time he was also attempting to translate *Malone meurt* (*Malone Dies*) and *L'Innommable* (*The Unnamable*) into English, and dealing with early productions of *Waiting for Godot*. Significantly, he also made a foray into dramatic mime, which may have helped him out of the creative bind. *Acte sans paroles* (*Act Without Words*) was written in 1955 for the dancer Deryk Mendel, who had solicited scenarios from a number of authors including Adamov, Beckett and Ionesco. John Beckett, the cousin of the author who had recently stayed with him in

Paris, was asked by Beckett to provide the musical accompaniment. Beckett's attraction to mime may have derived in part from his youthful interest in silent film, but it also surely stems from his attachment to shape, movement, repetition, precision and silence in the theatre. For one who made the failures of language a cardinal theme, the allure of mime is self-evident. Certainly we can see the mimic influence in the protracted dumbshow at the start of *Endgame*, when Clov prepares the scene by removing the sheets and uses the ladder to survey the world outside.

Beckett returned to his work on *Fin de partie* in early 1956, finishing a two-act version in February, but was not satisfied with it. A single, much longer act would more intently communicate an atmosphere of depletion, entropy and claustrophobia. The plan to stage the play together with *Acte sans paroles* in the Marseille Festival of the Avant-Garde in the coming August spurred him on. During April and May he reworked it closely, condensing it into one act and building in intricate variations and repetitions. On 21 June 1956, Beckett wrote to his American director and friend, Alan Schneider: 'Have at last written another, one act, longish, hour and a half, I fancy. Rather difficult and elliptical, mostly depending on the power of the text to claw, more inhuman than *Godot*.'[2]

This 'inhuman' quality derives from the terrible strictures of *Endgame*, spatial and temporal. The physical disabilities and mutilations of the characters mean that they cannot move freely, but the 'something' that is taking its course suggests they are also trapped in a deterministic or mechanical system. The fellow-feeling and flickers of compassion that uplift the bleak outlook of *Waiting for Godot* are, like so much else, in painfully short supply in *Endgame*. The relationships in *Endgame*, apart from one or two moments of geriatric romance between Nagg and Nell, are caustic and embittered. This is a play that is costive, scrupulous, remorseless, and seeks to articulate a vision whose only consolation, apart from its bitter humour, is its refusal to evade, distort or beguile.

In the event it was completed too late for the Marseille Festival to grant adequate rehearsal time. Both plays were withdrawn from the Festival and the search for a theatre in Paris began. Despite Beckett's success with *En attendant Godot*, this proved a greater challenge than might have been expected. A subvention had enabled production of the first play, but the commercial exigencies of theatre meant that, even in Paris, experimental drama could frighten theatre managers. As Beckett put it in a letter to his friend Thomas MacGreevy, 'With *Godot* after all, we had a State grant of 750,000 and now nothing but a gloomy graceless act, a complicated mime, and nos beaux yeux [our handsome eyes].'[3] Various Parisian theatres refused the play, and an arrangement with the Théâtre de l'Oeuvre fell through at the last moment. In an unusual twist for a play in French, the première of *Fin de partie* took place in London at the Royal Court Theatre on 3 April 1957 together with *Acte sans paroles*. Roger Blin, the French director and actor who had championed *Waiting for Godot* and to whom *Endgame* is dedicated, directed and played Hamm.

This initial production was generally received with hostility and bemusement. Even Kenneth Tynan, a prominent advocate for *Godot*, found its relentless bleakness forced and unconvincing. Many other British critics, apart from the perceptive Harold Hobson in *The Sunday Times*, were peevish about the seeming absence of hope. Pairing the play with *Acte sans paroles* seemed, in retrospect, to have been a mistake; Tynan acknowledged in his review that his response to *Fin de Partie* had been skewed by the 'facile pessimism' of the mime, which includes a player reaching in vain for a flask of water lowered from above only for it to be whisked away.[4]

After six performances in London, the production of *Fin de partie* moved to the Studio des Champs-Élysées in Paris, which had become available just after the Royal Court agreement had been signed. Because Beckett knew Blin so well, he became involved with the actors during the Royal Court Theatre run, and after the move to Paris. His concerns, and his disagreements with Blin, anticipated his future role as director of his own work. Here, as later, his instructions reveal a vision of the drama that is shaped and musical rather than actorly and dramatic. When Blin wanted to modulate Hamm's mode of address to Clov, rendering it, after an authoritarian beginning, weaker and more plaintive at the end, Beckett insisted that the voice be always on the same note, with the occasional shout. In other words he continually resisted the attempt to infuse the play with feeling. 'There is no drama whatsoever in *Fin de partie*,' he told Blin. 'There is a heap of words but no drama.'[5]

Beckett translated *Fin de partie* between May and August 1957, spurred on by the agreement he had made with George Devine of the English Stage Company, who had put on the French version in the Royal Court. It seems startling today, but until as recently as 1968 all commercial plays in the UK had to be approved for production by the Lord Chamberlain's office. This arrangement was always likely to irk Beckett, who was uncompromising about external interference in his work and deeply scornful of artistic censorship. When the play was sent for approval in December 1957, several changes were requested. Beckett, though he agreed to drop some words that were deemed objectionable ('balls' and 'arses') refused to emend the line about God in the prayer scene – 'The bastard! He doesn't exist!'. The licence was therefore initially refused. For this reason, the première of *Endgame* took place in New York's Cherry Lane Theater on 28 January 1958, directed by Beckett's preferred American director, Alan Schneider.

Beckett claimed that the prayer passage as it stood was indispensable. He made the intriguing defence (in a letter to Devine) that the line was 'no more blasphemous than "My God, my God, why hast Thou forsaken me?"'[6] The stalemate over the British production persisted for several months. A play that had been authorised for performance in French at the same theatre in the previous year, and had already been published in English in the UK, was now blocked because of official concerns about its blasphemous content. Arguments went on until the summer of 1958 when finally the word 'bastard' was replaced by 'swine', a compromise which Beckett regarded as a supreme concession on his part. The revised play was licensed for public perform-ance on 6 August. *Endgame* returned to the Royal Court Theatre in English on 28 October 1958 under the direction of Devine, who also played Hamm.

This Royal Court production marked a further stage in Beckett's progressive involvement with productions of his plays. He was in London chiefly to observe rehearsals for the new play, *Krapp's Last Tape*, as part of a double-bill, but he could not resist voicing concerns about *Endgame* to Devine after seeing a run-through that worried him. Again, Beckett edged the players away from interactions based on psychological or character-plausibility, dampening the efforts of Devine and Jack MacGowran, who played Clov (and would become one of Beckett's favoured actors), to develop the comedy in the Hamm–Clov relationship. Beckett ended up supervising the last few days of rehearsals, which may have been insufficient to realise what he had envisioned while at the same time impeding Devine's original intention. Again, British reviewers were not impressed, not least because many looked in vain for a repetition of the human solidarity in adversity that they had found in *Godot*.

Beckett always avoided first nights, loathing the attendant publicity and exposure. But his companion (later his wife) Suzanne Deschevaux-Dumesnil often went in his stead and duly reported back on the efficacy or otherwise of the produc-tion and the audience reaction. Famously, Beckett claimed not to be able to give privileged information or insights into the 'meaning' of his plays. But nor was he the sort of playwright who sent his plays off to make their own way in the world, or allowed directors to bend and innovate as they saw fit. He exerted fastidious control over productions during his lifetime, blocking plans for experimental stagings that tampered with the script or deviated from the stage directions. The Beckett Estate has, often controversially, continued the effort to abide strictly by the author's intentions.

In a sense, Beckett's scruple about deviation in productions of his work is embryonic in the plays themselves, marked as they are by meticulous exactitude. This meticulousness carried over into his directorial collaborations with Blin, Devine and Schneider on the early stagings of *Endgame* and, later, when he came to direct the play himself. If Beckett's interventions in his plays during their production complicate our sense of where the act of creation begins and ends, so too does his involvement during the process of translation. Which is the primary or authoritative text: the original French version or its English translation? Beckett complained in correspondence about the necessary compromises and distortions of translation. On the other hand, his English *Endgame* tweaks and omits scenes from *Fin de partie*, not least because he had the benefit of seeing the play in production before attempting to translate it. Significantly enough, the changes made to the typescript during his own direction of the play for the Schiller-Theater in Berlin (1967) bring the text closer to the English version.[7] In this production he strove to make things tauter, excluding elements that could be deemed superfluous, like the short verse that Clov sings in the French version (but not in the English). In his own productions Beckett notably dispensed with the initial stage directions specifying that Clov and Hamm have very red faces and Nagg and Nell very white ones. Most productions have followed suit, though the stage direction remains in the printed text.

Beckett also simplified the mimes when he directed in Berlin, and in the Riverside Studios in London in 1980, cutting back both on Clov's initial dumbshow and his later inspections through the window. But this should not be regarded as a lessening of his interest in the visual aspects of dramatic presentation. Perhaps the most famous decision by Beckett in his Schiller-Theater production was his request to the actors to forego the curtain call, in order to preserve the final tableau of Clov ready to leave, but not yet having done so: 'It would have hurt me to break up the picture at the end,' he confessed.[8] Beckett's need to preserve that final picture indicates, for all his attempts to rupture realist convention in the theatre, a deep sense of the integrity of the dramatic art. He is reluctant to release its discipline even at the very end, reluctant to restore the reassuring schism between art and life by allowing the tacit admission of illusion that a curtain call implies.

II

Many of the critics of the first productions of *Endgame* were dismayed by the bleak and unremitting philosophy they discerned in the play. Beckett, on the other hand, did not consider himself a philosophical writer. The idea that *Endgame* has some message or moral that can be readily distilled from the dramatic action is one that is explicitly denied by the play:

> HAMM: We're not beginning to . . . to . . . mean something?
> CLOV: Mean something! You and I, mean something! [*Brief laugh.*] Ah that's a good one!

Later critics, notably the German philosopher Theodor Adorno, lauded in Beckett precisely this recalcitrance, whose challenge to orthodox values and their grammar of understanding seemed appropriate to the crisis of culture and confidence after the Second World War. If civilization could lead to such barbarism, it seemed necessary to overhaul and renovate it, including its artistic and literary heritage. The allusions in *Endgame* to the pinnacles of the Western literary canon, to the Bible, Shakespeare, Sophocles and numerous others, bob around the text like the flotsam of a wrecked tradition. In a famous essay on the play, Adorno praises *Endgame* for dramatising an incoherent situation without thereby losing the sense of incoherence: 'To understand *Endgame* can only mean understanding why it cannot be understood.'[9] Rather than asserting an abstract message, *Endgame* thwarts those faculties of understanding that seek out such easily digestible fare. Often it does so precisely by under-delivering on dramatic expectation, by deploying inaction, even boredom, to estrange the audience. Rather than simply asserting an absence of meaning, the play strives to demonstrate and embody this absence. Whereas in abstract philosophy, what we understand occurs at the level of ideas, *Endgame* claws at deeper and darker levels of experience and intuition. Harold Hobson, amongst the early reviewers, perhaps came closest to understanding this aspect of the play when he wrote in his review of *Fin de Partie*: 'Mr Beckett is a poet; and the business of a poet is not to clarify, but to suggest, to imply, to employ words with auras of association, with a reaching out towards a vision, a probing down into an emotion, beyond the compass of explicit definition.'[10]

This lack of geographical and temporal certainty have often led Beckett's interpreters to discern a universal or ahistorical vision of the human condition here and in his other plays. Yet, for all its seeming rootlessness, Beckett's world is a product of its place and time, bearing testament to a particular historical moment. Thus despite the absence of overt references to the Second World War in his work, it deeply scoured his imagination. Beckett witnessed suffering and devastation at first hand and lost some of his closest friends; he was active in the Resistance in Paris and went into hiding in Vichy France after his cell was betrayed. The plays and novels that he wrote during his creative upsurge immediately after the war are hard to imagine without the experiences of those five years.

Critics have variously identified the barren world through the windows with post-nuclear apocalypse, the devastations of the Holocaust or the ravaged Normandy landscape that Beckett drove through in 1945, as a volunteer ambulance driver for the Irish Red Cross. More biographically, *Endgame*'s atmosphere of death and desolation is a register of the bereavement that Beckett suffered around the time of its composition. In May 1954 Beckett discovered that his brother Frank was suffering from terminal lung cancer. He immediately returned to Dublin and spent the summer with Frank and his family. 'And so soon it will have been another day and all the secret things inside a little worse than they were and nothing much noticed,' he wrote in a letter to Pamela Mitchell.[11] Frank's illness and death, on 13 September 1954, caused Beckett terrible anguish, surely evident in the preoccupation with 'ending' that haunts this play.

Yet *Endgame* is not autobiography and, like much of Beckett's work, it deliberately withholds clarity and certainty of reference, just as it withholds allegiance to any of the postwar attempts to process modern historical experience, such as the widely influential philosophy of 'the absurd' (borrowing from the existentialist Albert Camus), towards which Beckett expressed misgivings: 'I have never accepted the notion of a theatre of the absurd, a concept that implies a judgement of value. It's not even possible to talk about truth. That's part of the anguish.'[12] In *Endgame*, it is not just the material things, the painkillers, sugar plums and bicycle wheels, which are running scarce. Less effable, but more fundamental, is the erosion of meaning, of the value-system which a sense of tragedy as such requires. In *Endgame*, parents are kept in rubbish bins, the death of a mother is scarcely due a mention, and the sight of a child prompts a murderous response. There are certainly layers of parody and black comedy in the depiction of Hamm's attitude to his parents (as indeed there is in his horror at the prospect of evolution starting all over again). But there is also a strongly subversive and shocking refusal of the values of life, the family, and 'progress'. By its refusals, *Endgame* brings the oldest and most venerated literary mode of the Western tradition – dramatic tragedy – into a belated and bewildered modernity.

Notes

1 Kenneth Tynan in the *Observer*, 7 August 1955. Reprinted in Lawrence Graver and Raymond Federman (eds), *Samuel Beckett: The Critical Heritage* (London and Boston: Routledge and Kegan Paul, 1979), p. 97.
2 Maurice Harmon (ed.), *No Author Better Served: The Correspondence of Samuel Beckett and Alan Schneider* (Cambridge MA and London: Harvard University Press, 1998), p. 11.

3 Quoted in James Knowlson, *Damned to Fame: The Life of Samuel Beckett* (London: Bloomsbury, 1996), p. 425

4 Tynan in the *Observer*, 7 April 1957. Reprinted in Graver and Federman, *The Critical Heritage*, p. 166.

5 Quoted in Anthony Cronin, *Samuel Beckett: The Last Modernist* (London: HarperCollins, 1996), p. 466.

6 Samuel Beckett to George Devine, 26 December 1957. Quoted in Knowlson, *Damned to Fame*, p. 449.

7 *The Theatrical Notebooks of Samuel Beckett*, Gen. Ed. James Knowlson, Vol II: *Endgame*, ed. S. E. Gontarski (London: Faber and Faber, 1992), p. xviii.

8 Quoted in ibid., p. 71.

9 Theodor W. Adorno, 'Towards an Understanding of *Endgame*', trans. Samuel M. Weber [originally 'Versuch, das Endspiel zu verstehen' (1961)] in Bell Gale Chevigny (ed.), *Twentieth Century Interpretations of 'Endgame'* (Englewood Cliffs, NJ: Prentice Hall, 1969), p. 84.

10 Harold Hobson, the *Sunday Times*, 7 April 1957. Reprinted in Graver and Federman, *The Critical Heritage*, p. 162.

11 Undated letter to Pamela Mitchell, probably mid-June 1954. Quoted in Knowlson, *Damned to Fame*, p. 402.

12 Charles Juliet, 'Meeting Beckett', trans. and ed. Suzanne Chamier, *TriQuarterly* 77 (Winter, 1989–90, p. 17. An extract from *Rencontres avec Samuel Beckett* (Saint-Clément-la-Rivière: Editions Fata Morgana, 1986).

Table of Dates

[Note: where unspecified, translations from French to English or vice versa are by Beckett]

1906

13 April   Samuel Beckett [Samuel Barclay Beckett] born at 'Cooldrinagh', a house in Foxrock, a village south of Dublin, on Good Friday, the second child of William Beckett and May Beckett, née Roe; he is preceded by a brother, Frank Edward, born 26 July 1902.

1911

Enters kindergarten at Ida and Pauline Elsner's private academy in Leopardstown.

1915

Attends larger Earlsfort House School in Dublin.

1920

Follows Frank to Portora Royal, a distinguished Protestant boarding school in Enniskillen, County Fermanagh (soon to become part of Northern Ireland).

1923

October   Enrolls at Trinity College, Dublin (TCD) to study for an Arts degree.

1926

August   First visit to France, a month-long cycling tour of the Loire Valley.

1927

April–August   Travels through Florence and Venice, visiting museums, galleries, and churches.

December   Receives B.A. in Modern Languages (French and Italian) and graduates first in the First Class.

1928

Jan.–June — Teaches French and English at Campbell College, Belfast.

September — First trip to Germany to visit seventeen-year-old Peggy Sinclair, a cousin on his father's side, and her family in Kassel.

1 November — Arrives in Paris as an exchange *lecteur* at the École Normale Supérieure. Quickly becomes friends with his predecessor, Thomas MacGreevy, who introduces Beckett to James Joyce and other influential Anglophone writers and publishers.

December — Spends Christmas in Kassel (as also in 1929, 1930, and 1931).

1929

June — Publishes first critical essay ('Dante . . . Bruno. Vico . . Joyce') and first story ('Assumption') in *transition* magazine.

1930

July — *Whoroscope* (Paris: Hours Press).

October — Returns to TCD to begin a two-year appointment as lecturer in French.

November — Introduced by MacGreevy to the painter and writer Jack B. Yeats in Dublin.

1931

March — *Proust* (London: Chatto and Windus).

September — First Irish publication, the poem 'Alba' in *Dublin Magazine*.

1932

January — Resigns his lectureship via telegram from Kassel and moves to Paris.

Feb.–June — First serious attempt at a novel, the posthumously published *Dream of Fair to Middling Women*.

December — Story 'Dante and the Lobster' appears in *This Quarter* (Paris).

1933

3 May	Death of Peggy Sinclair from tuberculosis.
26 June	Death of William Beckett from a heart attack.

1934

January	Moves to London and begins psychoanalysis with Wilfred Bion at the Tavistock Clinic.
February	*Negro Anthology*, edited by Nancy Cunard and with numerous translations by Beckett (London: Wishart and Company).
May	*More Pricks Than Kicks* (London: Chatto and Windus).
Aug.–Sept.	Contributes several stories and reviews to literary magazines in London and Dublin.

1935

November	*Echo's Bones and Other Precipitates*, a cycle of thirteen poems (Paris: Europa Press).

1936

	Returns to Dublin.
29 September	Leaves Ireland for a seven-month stay in Germany.

1937

Apr.–Aug.	First serious attempt at a play, *Human Wishes*, about Samuel Johnson and his circle.
October	Settles in Paris.

1938

6/7 January	Stabbed by a street pimp in Montparnasse. Among his visitors at L'Hôpital Broussais is Suzanne Deschevaux-Dumesnil, an acquaintance who is to become Beckett's companion for life.
March	*Murphy* (London: Routledge).
April	Begins writing poetry directly in French.

1939

3 September	Great Britain and France declare war on Germany. Beckett abruptly ends a visit to Ireland and returns to Paris the next day.

1940

June — Travels south with Suzanne following the Fall of France, as part of the exodus from the capital.

September — Returns to Paris.

1941

13 January — Death of James Joyce in Zurich.

1 September — Joins the Resistance cell Gloria SMH.

1942

16 August — Goes into hiding with Suzanne after the arrest of close friend Alfred Péron.

6 October — Arrival at Roussillon, a small unoccupied village in Vichy France.

1944

24 August — Liberation of Paris.

1945

30 March — Awarded the Croix de Guerre.

Aug.–Dec. — Volunteers as a storekeeper and interpreter with the Irish Red Cross in St-Lô, Normandy.

1946

July — Publishes first fiction in French – a truncated version of the short story 'Suite' (later to become 'La Fin') in *Les Temps modernes*, owing to a misunderstanding with editors – as well as a critical essay on Dutch painters Geer and Bram van Velde in *Cahiers d'art*.

1947

Jan.–Feb. — Writes first play, in French, *Eleutheria* (published posthumously).

April — *Murphy* translated into French (Paris: Bordas).

1948

Undertakes a number of translations commissioned by UNESCO and by Georges Duthuit.

1950

25 August   Death of May Beckett.

1951

March   *Molloy*, in French (Paris: Les Éditions de Minuit).

November   *Malone meurt* (Paris: Minuit).

1952

     Purchases land at Ussy-sur-Marne, subsequently Beckett's preferred location for writing.

September   *En attendant Godot* (Paris: Minuit).

1953

5 January   Premiere of *Godot* at the Théâtre de Babylone in Montparnasse, directed by Roger Blin.

May   *L'Innommable* (Paris: Minuit).

August   *Watt*, in English (Paris: Olympia Press).

1954

8 September   *Waiting for Godot* (New York: Grove Press).

13 September   Death of Frank Beckett from lung cancer.

1955

March   *Molloy*, translated into English with Patrick Bowles (New York: Grove; Paris: Olympia).

3 August   First English production of *Godot* opens in London at the Arts Theatre.

November   *Nouvelles et Textes pour rien* (Paris: Minuit).

1956

3 January   American *Godot* premiere in Miami.

February   First British publication of *Waiting for Godot* (London: Faber).

October   *Malone Dies* (New York: Grove).

1957

January   First radio broadcast, *All That Fall* on the BBC Third Programme.

     Fin de partie, suivi de Acte sans paroles (Paris: Minuit).

28 March   Death of Jack B. Yeats.

August	*All That Fall* (London: Faber).
October	*Tous ceux qui tombent,* translation of *All That Fall* with Robert Pinget (Paris: Minuit).
1958	
April	*Endgame,* translation of *Fin de partie* (London: Faber).
	From an Abandoned Work (London: Faber).
July	*Krapp's Last Tape* in Grove Press's literary magazine, *Evergreen Review.*
September	*The Unnamable* (New York: Grove).
December	*Anthology of Mexican Poetry,* translated by Beckett (Bloomington: Indiana University Press; later reprinted in London by Thames and Hudson).
1959	
March	*La Dernière bande,* translation of *Krapp's Last Tape* with Pierre Leyris, in the Parisian literary magazine *Les Lettres nouvelles.*
2 July	Receives honorary D.Litt. degree from Trinity College, Dublin.
November	*Embers* in *Evergreen Review.*
December	*Cendres,* translation of *Embers* with Pinget, in *Les Lettres nouvelles.*
	Three Novels: Molloy, Malone Dies, The Unnamable (New York: Grove; Paris: Olympia Press).
1961	
January	*Comment c'est* (Paris: Minuit).
24 March	Marries Suzanne at Folkestone, Kent.
May	Shares Prix International des Editeurs with Jorge Luis Borges.
August	*Poems in English* (London: Calder).
September	*Happy Days* (New York: Grove).
1963	
February	*Oh les beaux jours,* translation of *Happy Days* (Paris: Minuit).

May	Assists with the German production of *Play* (*Spiel*, translated by Elmar and Erika Tophoven) in Ulm.
22 May	Outline of *Film* sent to Grove Press. *Film* would be produced in 1964, starring Buster Keaton, and released at the Venice Film Festival the following year.

1964

March	*Play and Two Short Pieces for Radio* (London: Faber).
April	*How It Is*, translation of *Comment c'est* (London: Calder; New York: Grove).
June	*Comédie*, translation of *Play*, in *Les Lettres nouvelles*.
July–Aug.	First and only trip to the United States, to assist with the production of *Film* in New York.

1965

October	*Imagination morte imaginez* (Paris: Minuit).
November	*Imagination Dead Imagine* (London: *The Sunday Times*, Calder).

1966

January	*Comédie et Actes divers*, including *Dis Joe* and *Va et vient* (Paris: Minuit).
February	*Assez* (Paris: Minuit).
October	*Bing* (Paris: Minuit).

1967

February	*D'un ouvrage abandonné* (Paris: Minuit). *Têtes-mortes* (Paris: Minuit).
16 March	Death of Thomas MacGreevy.
June	*Eh Joe and Other Writings*, including *Act Without Words II* and *Film* (London: Faber).
July	*Come and Go*, English translation of *Va et vient* (London: Calder).
26 September	Directs first solo production, *Endspiel* (translation of *Endgame* by Elmar Tophoven) in Berlin.

production of *Godot*, directed by Walter
Asmus, in London.
Collected Shorter Plays (London: Faber; New
York: Grove).

May	*Collected Poems 1930–1978* (London: Calder).
July	*Collected Shorter Prose 1945–1980* (London: Calder).
1989	
April	*Stirrings Still* (New York: Blue Moon Books).
June	*Nohow On: Company, Ill Seen Ill Said, Worstward Ho*, illustrated with etchings by Robert Ryman (New York: Limited Editions Club).
July 17	Death of Suzanne Beckett.
December 22	Death of Samuel Beckett. Burial in Cimetière de Montparnasse.
1990	
	As the Story Was Told: Uncollected and Late Prose (London: Calder; New York: Riverrun Press).
1992	
	Dream of Fair to Middling Women (Dublin: Black Cat Press).
1995	
	Eleutheria (Paris: Minuit).
1996	
	Eleutheria, translated into English by Barbara Wright (London: Faber).
1998	
	No Author Better Served: The Correspondence of Samuel Beckett and Alan Schneider, edited by Maurice Harmon (Cambridge: Harvard University Press).
2000	
	Beckett on Film: nineteen films, by different

directors, of Beckett's works for the stage (RTÉ, Channel 4, and Irish Film Board; DVD, London: Clarence Pictures).

2006

Samuel Beckett: Works for Radio: The Original Broadcasts: five works spanning the period 1957–1976 (CD, London: British Library Board).

Compiled by Cassandra Nelson

5

Manuscript draft of *Fin de partie* (*Endgame*)
Courtesy of the Beckett International Foundation, University of Reading.
© The Estate of Samuel Beckett.

Endgame

For Roger Blin

CHARACTERS

HAMM
CLOV
NAGG
NELL

Bare interior.

Grey light.

Left and right back, high up, two small windows, curtains drawn.
Front right, a door. Hanging near door, its face to wall, a picture.
Front left, touching each other, covered with an old sheet, two
ashbins.

Centre, in an armchair on castors, covered with an old sheet,
HAMM.

Motionless by the door, his eyes fixed on HAMM, CLOV. *Very red*
face.

Brief tableau.

CLOV *goes and stands under window left. Stiff, staggering walk.*
He looks up at window left. He turns and looks at window right.
He goes and stands under window right. He looks up at window
right. He turns and looks at window left. He goes out, comes back
immediately with a small step-ladder, carries it over and sets it
down under window left, gets up on it, draws back curtain. He gets
down, takes six steps [for example] towards window right, goes back
for ladder, carries it over and sets it down under window right, gets
up on it, draws back curtain. He gets down, takes three steps
towards window left, goes back for ladder, carries it over and sets it
down under window left, gets up on it, looks out of window. Brief
laugh. He gets down, takes one step towards window right, goes back
for ladder, carries it over and sets it down under window right, gets
up on it, looks out of window. Brief laugh. He gets down, goes with
ladder towards ashbins, halts, turns, carries back ladder and sets it
down under window right, goes to ashbins, removes sheet covering
them, folds it over his arm. He raises one lid, stoops and looks into
bin. Brief laugh. He closes lid. Same with other bin. He goes to
HAMM, *removes sheet covering him, folds it over his arm. In a*

dressing-gown, a stiff toque on his head, a large blood-stained handkerchief over his face, a whistle hanging from his neck, a rug over his knees, thick socks on his feet, HAMM *seems to be asleep.* CLOV *looks him over. Brief laugh. He goes to door, halts, turns towards auditorium.*

CLOV: [*Fixed gaze, tonelessly.*] Finished, it's finished, nearly finished, it must be nearly finished. [*Pause.*] Grain upon grain, one by one, and one day, suddenly, there's a heap, a little heap, the impossible heap. [*Pause.*] I can't be punished any more. [*Pause.*] I'll go now to my kitchen, ten feet by ten feet by ten feet, and wait for him to whistle me. [*Pause.*] Nice dimensions, nice proportions, I'll lean on the table, and look at the wall, and wait for him to whistle me. [*He remains a moment motionless, then goes out. He comes back immediately, goes to window right, takes up the ladder and carries it out. Pause.* HAMM *stirs. He yawns under the handkerchief. He removes the. handkerchief from his face. Very red face. Black glasses.*]

HAMM: Me – [*he yawns*] – to play. [*He holds the handkerchief spread out before him.*] Old stancher! [*He takes off his glasses, wipes his eyes, his face, the glasses, puts them on again, folds the handkerchief and puts it neatly in the breast-pocket of his dressing-gown. He clears his throat, joins the tips of his fingers.*] Can there be misery – [*he yawns*] – loftier than mine? No doubt. Formerly. But now? [*Pause.*] My father? [*Pause.*] My mother? [*Pause.*] My . . . dog? [*Pause.*] Oh I am willing to believe they suffer as much as such creatures can suffer. But does that mean their sufferings equal mine? No doubt. [*Pause.*] No, all is a – [*he yawns*] – bsolute, [*proudly*] the bigger a man is the fuller he is. [*Pause. Gloomily.*] And the emptier. [*He sniffs.*] Clov! [*Pause.*] No, alone. [*Pause.*] What dreams! Those forests! [*Pause.*] Enough, it's time it ended, in the refuge too. [*Pause.*] And yet I hesitate, I hesitate to . . . to end. Yes, there it is, it's time it ended and yet I hesitate to – [*he yawns*] – to end. [*Yawns.*] God, I'm tired, I'd be better off in bed. [*He whistles. Enter* CLOV *immediately. He halts beside the chair.*] You pollute the air [*Pause.*] Get me ready, I'm going to bed.

CLOV: I've just got you up.

HAMM: And what of it?

CLOV: I can't be getting you up and putting you to bed every five minutes, I have things to do.
[*Pause.*]

HAMM: Did you ever see my eyes?

CLOV: No.

HAMM: Did you never have the curiosity, while I was sleeping, to take off my glasses and look at my eyes?

CLOV: Pulling back the lids? [*Pause.*] No.

HAMM: One of these days I'll show them to you. [*Pause.*] It seems they've gone all white. [*Pause.*] What time is it?

CLOV: The same as usual.

HAMM: [*Gesture towards window right.*] Have you looked?

CLOV: Yes.

HAMM: Well?

CLOV: Zero.

HAMM: It'd need to rain.

CLOV: It won't rain.
[*Pause.*]

HAMM: Apart from that, how do you feel?

CLOV: I don't complain.

HAMM: You feel normal?

CLOV: [*Irritably.*] I tell you I don't complain!

HAMM: I feel a little queer. [*Pause.*] Clov!

CLOV: Yes.

HAMM: Have you not had enough?

CLOV: Yes! [*Pause.*] Of what?

HAMM: Of this . . . this . . . thing.

CLOV: I always had. [*Pause.*] Not you?

HAMM: [*Gloomily.*] Then there's no reason for it to change.

CLOV: It may end. [*Pause.*] All life long the same questions, the same answers.

HAMM: Get me ready. [CLOV *does not move.*] Go and get the
sheet. [CLOV *does not move.*] Clov!

CLOV: Yes.

HAMM: I'll give you nothing more to eat.

CLOV: Then we'll die.

HAMM: I'll give you just enough to keep you from dying.
You'll be hungry all the time.

CLOV: Then we shan't die. [*Pause.*] I'll go and get the sheet.
[*He goes towards the door.*]

HAMM: No! [CLOV *halts.*] I'll give you one biscuit per day.
[*Pause.*] One and a half. [*Pause.*] Why do you stay with
me?

CLOV: Why do you keep me?

HAMM: There's no one else.

CLOV: There's nowhere else.
[*Pause.*]

HAMM: You're leaving me all the same.

CLOV: I'm trying.

HAMM: You don't love me.

CLOV: No.

HAMM: You loved me once.

CLOV: Once!

HAMM: I've made you suffer too much. [*Pause.*] Haven't I?

CLOV: It's not that.

HAMM: [*Shocked.*] I haven't made you suffer too much?

CLOV: Yes!

HAMM: [*Relieved.*] Ah you gave me a fright! [*Pause. Coldly.*]
Forgive me. [*Pause. Louder.*] I said, Forgive me.

CLOV: I heard you. [*Pause.*] Have you bled?

HAMM: Less. [*Pause.*] Is it not time for my pain-killer?

CLOV: No.
[*Pause.*]

HAMM: How are your eyes?

CLOV: Bad.

HAMM: How are your legs?

CLOV: Bad.

HAMM: But you can move.

CLOV: Yes.

HAMM: [*Violently.*] Then move! [CLOV *goes to back wall, leans against it with his forehead and hands.*] Where are you?

CLOV: Here.

HAMM: Come back! [CLOV *returns to his place beside the chair.*] Where are you?

CLOV: Here.

HAMM: Why don't you kill me?

CLOV: I don't know the combination of the larder.
   [*Pause.*]

HAMM: Go and get two bicycle-wheels.

CLOV: There are no more bicycle-wheels.

HAMM: What have you done with your bicycle?

CLOV: I never had a bicycle.

HAMM: The thing is impossible.

CLOV: When there were still bicycles I wept to have one. I crawled at your feet. You told me to get out to hell. Now there are none.

HAMM: And your rounds? When you inspected my paupers. Always on foot?

CLOV: Sometimes on horse. [*The lid of one of the bins lifts and the hands of* NAGG *appear, gripping the rim. Then his head emerges. Nightcap. Very white face.* NAGG *yawns, then listens.*] I'll leave you, I have things to do.

HAMM: In your kitchen?

CLOV: Yes.

HAMM: Outside of here it's death. [*Pause.*] All right, be off. [*Exit* CLOV. *Pause.*] We're getting on.

NAGG: Me pap!

HAMM: Accursed progenitor!

NAGG: Me pap!

HAMM: The old folks at home! No decency left! Guzzle, guzzle, that's all they think of. [*He whistles. Enter* CLOV. *He halts beside the chair.*] Well! I thought you were leaving me.

CLOV: Oh not just yet, not just yet.

NAGG: Me pap!

HAMM: Give him his pap.

CLOV: There's no more pap.

HAMM: [*To* NAGG.] Do you hear that? There's no more pap. You'll never get any more pap.

NAGG: I want me pap!

HAMM: Give him a biscuit. [*Exit* CLOV.] Accursed fornicator! How are your stumps?

NAGG: Never mind me stumps.

[*Enter* CLOV *with biscuit.*]

CLOV: I'm back again, with the biscuit.

[*He gives the biscuit to* NAGG *who fingers it, sniffs it.*]

NAGG: [*Plaintively.*] What is it?

CLOV: Spratt's medium.

NAGG: [*As before.*] It's hard! I can't!

HAMM: Bottle him!

[CLOV *pushes* NAGG *back into the bin, closes the lid.*]

CLOV: [*Returning to his place beside the chair.*] If age but knew!

HAMM: Sit on him!

CLOV: I can't sit.

HAMM: True. And I can't stand.

CLOV: So it is.

HAMM: Every man his speciality. [*Pause.*] No phone calls? [*Pause.*] Don't we laugh?

CLOV: [*After reflection.*] I don't feel like it.

HAMM: [*After reflection.*] Nor I. [*Pause.*] Clov!

CLOV: Yes.

HAMM: Nature has forgotten us.

CLOV: There's no more nature.

HAMM: No more nature! You exaggerate.

CLOV: In the vicinity.

HAMM: But we breathe, we change! We lose our hair, our teeth! Our bloom! Our ideals!

CLOV: Then she hasn't forgotten us.

HAMM: But you say there is none.

CLOV: [*Sadly.*] No one that ever lived ever thought so
     crooked as we.

HAMM: We do what we can.

CLOV: We shouldn't.
     [*Pause.*]

HAMM: You're a bit of all right, aren't you?

CLOV: A smithereen.
     [*Pause.*]

HAMM: This is slow work. [*Pause.*] Is it not time for my
     pain-killer?

CLOV: No. [*Pause.*] I'll leave you, I have things to do.

HAMM: In your kitchen?

CLOV: Yes.

HAMM: What, I'd like to know.

CLOV: I look at the wall.

HAMM: The wall! And what do you see on your wall? Mene,
     mene? Naked bodies?

CLOV: I see my light dying.

HAMM: Your light dying! Listen to that! Well, it can die just
     as well here, *your* light. Take a look at me and then come
     back and tell me what you think of *your* light.
     [*Pause.*]

CLOV: You shouldn't speak to me like that.
     [*Pause.*]

HAMM: [*Coldly.*] Forgive me. [*Pause. Louder.*] I said,
     Forgive me.

CLOV: I heard you.
     [*The lid of* NAGG's *bin lifts. His hands appear, gripping the
     rim. Then his head emerges. In his mouth the biscuit. He
     listens.*]

HAMM: Did your seeds come up?

CLOV: No.

HAMM: Did you scratch round them to see if they had
     sprouted?

CLOV: They haven't sprouted.

HAMM: Perhaps it's still too early.

CLOV: If they were going to sprout they would have sprouted. [*Violently.*] They'll never sprout.
[*Pause.* NAGG *takes biscuit in his hand.*]

HAMM: This is not much fun. [*Pause.*] But that's always the way at the end of the day, isn't it, Clov?

CLOV: Always.

HAMM: It's the end of the day like any other day, isn't it, Clov?

CLOV: Looks like it.
[*Pause.*]

HAMM: [*Anguished.*] What's happening, what's happening?

CLOV: Something is taking its course.
[*Pause.*]

HAMM: All right, be off. [*He leans back in his chair, remains motionless.* CLOV *does not move, heaves a great groaning sigh.* HAMM *sits up.*] I thought I told you to be off.

CLOV: I'm trying. [*He goes to door, halts.*] Ever since I was whelped.
[*Exit* CLOV.]

HAMM: We're getting on.
[*He leans back in his chair, remains motionless.* NAGG *knocks on the lid of the other bin. Pause. He knocks harder. The lid lifts and the hands of* NELL *appear, gripping the rim. Then her head emerges. Lace cap. Very white face.*]

NELL: What is it, my pet? [*Pause.*] Time for love?

NAGG: Were you asleep?

NELL: Oh no!

NAGG: Kiss me.

NELL: We can't.

NAGG: Try.
[*Their heads strain towards each other, fail to meet, fall apart again.*]

NELL: Why this farce, day after day?
[*Pause.*]

NAGG: I've lost me tooth.

NELL: When?

NAGG: I had it yesterday.

NELL: [*Elegiac.*] Ah yesterday!

[*They turn painfully towards each other.*]

NAGG: Can you see me?

NELL: Hardly. And you?

NAGG: What?

NELL: Can you see me?

NAGG: Hardly.

NELL: So much the better, so much the better.

NAGG: Don't say that. [*Pause.*] Our sight has failed.

NELL: Yes.

[*Pause. They turn away from each other.*]

NAGG: Can you hear me?

NELL: Yes. And you?

NAGG: Yes. [*Pause.*] Our hearing hasn't failed.

NELL: Our what?

NAGG: Our hearing.

NELL: No. [*Pause.*] Have you anything else to say to me?

NAGG: Do you remember–

NELL: No.

NAGG: When we crashed on our tandem and lost our shanks.

[*They laugh heartily.*]

NELL: It was in the Ardennes.

[*They laugh less heartily.*]

NAGG: On the road to Sedan. [*They laugh still less heartily.*]
Are you cold?

NELL: Yes, perished. And you?

NAGG: I'm freezing. [*Pause.*] Do you want to go in?

NELL: Yes.

NAGG: Then go in. [NELL *does not move.*] Why don't you go in?

NELL: I don't know.

[*Pause.*]

NAGG: Has he changed your sawdust?

NELL: It isn't sawdust. [*Pause. Wearily.*] Can you not be a
little accurate, Nagg?

NAGG: Your sand then. It's not important.

NELL: It is important.

[*Pause.*]

NAGG: It was sawdust once.

NELL: Once!

NAGG: And now it's sand. [*Pause.*] From the shore.
[*Pause. Impatiently.*] Now it's sand he fetches from the
shore.

NELL: Now it's sand.

NAGG: Has he changed yours?

NELL: No.

NAGG: Nor mine. [*Pause.*] I won't have it! [*Pause. Holding up
the biscuit.*] Do you want a bit?

NELL: No. [*Pause.*] Of what?

NAGG: Biscuit. I've kept you half. [*He looks at the biscuit.
Proudly.*] Three quarters. For you. Here. [*He proffers the
biscuit.*] No? [*Pause.*] Do you not feel well?

HAMM: [*Wearily.*] Quiet, quiet, you're keeping me awake.
[*Pause.*] Talk softer. [*Pause.*] If I could sleep I might make
love. I'd go into the woods. My eyes would see . . . the
sky, the earth. I'd run, run, they wouldn't catch me.
[*Pause.*] Nature! [*Pause.*] There's something dripping in
my head. [*Pause.*] A heart, a heart in my head.
[*Pause.*]

NAGG: [*Soft.*] Do you hear him? A heart in his head!
[*He chuckles cautiously.*]

NELL: One musn't laugh at those things, Nagg. Why must
you always laugh at them?

NAGG: Not so loud!

NELL: [*Without lowering her voice.*] Nothing is funnier than
unhappiness, I grant you that. But–

NAGG: [*Shocked.*] Oh!

NELL: Yes, yes, it's the most comical thing in the world. And
we laugh, we laugh, with a will, in the beginning. But it's
always the same thing. Yes, it's like the funny story we have
heard too often, we still find it funny, but we don't laugh
any more. [*Pause.*] Have you anything else to say to me?

NAGG: No.

NELL: Are you quite sure? [*Pause.*] Then I'll leave you.

NAGG: Do you not want your biscuit? [*Pause.*] I'll keep it for you. [*Pause.*] I thought you were going to leave me.

NELL: I am going to leave you.

NAGG: Could you give me a scratch before you go?

NELL: No. [*Pause.*] Where?

NAGG: In the back.

NELL: No. [*Pause.*] Rub yourself against the rim.

NAGG: It's lower down. In the hollow.

NELL: What hollow?

NAGG: The hollow! [*Pause.*] Could you not? [*Pause.*] Yesterday you scratched me there.

NELL: [*Elegiac.*] Ah yesterday!

NAGG: Could you not? [*Pause.*] Would you like me to scratch you? [*Pause.*] Are you crying again?

NELL: I was trying.

[*Pause.*]

HAMM: Perhaps it's a little vein.

[*Pause.*]

NAGG: What was that he said?

NELL: Perhaps it's a little vein.

NAGG: What does that mean? [*Pause.*] That means nothing. [*Pause.*] Will I tell you the story of the tailor?

NELL: No. [*Pause.*] What for?

NAGG: To cheer you up.

NELL: It's not funny.

NAGG: It always made you laugh. [*Pause.*] The first time I thought you'd die.

NELL: It was on Lake Como. [*Pause.*] One April afternoon. [*Pause.*] Can you believe it?

NAGG: What?

NELL: That we once went out rowing on Lake Como. [*Pause.*] One April afternoon.

NAGG: We had got engaged the day before.

NELL: Engaged!

NAGG: You were in such fits that we capsized. By rights we should have been drowned.

NELL: It was because I felt happy.

NAGG: [*Indignant.*] It was not, it was my story and nothing else. Happy! Don't you laugh at it still? Every time I tell it. Happy!

NELL: It was deep, deep. And you could see down to the bottom. So white. So clean.

NAGG: Let me tell it again. [*Raconteur's voice.*] An Englishman, needing a pair of striped trousers in a hurry for the New Year festivities, goes to his tailor who takes his measurements. [*Tailor's voice.*] 'That's the lot, come back in four days, I'll have it ready.' Good. Four days later. [*Tailor's voice.*] 'So sorry, come back in a week, I've made a mess of the seat.' Good, that's all right, a neat seat can be very ticklish. A week later. [*Tailor's voice.*] 'Frightfully sorry, come back in ten days, I've made a hash of the crutch.' Good, can't be helped, a snug crutch is always a teaser. Ten days later. [*Tailor's voice.*] 'Dreadfully sorry, come back in a fortnight, I've made a balls of the fly.' Good, at a pinch, a smart fly is a stiff proposition. [*Pause. Normal voice.*] I never told it worse. [*Pause. Gloomy.*] I tell this story worse and worse. [*Pause. Raconteur's voice.*] Well, to make it short, the bluebells are blowing and he ballockses the buttonholes. [*Customer's voice.*] 'God damn you to hell, Sir, no, it's indecent, there are limits! In six days, do you hear me, six days, God made the world. Yes Sir, no less Sir, the WORLD! And you are not bloody well capable of making me a pair of trousers in three months!' [*Tailor's voice, scandalized.*] 'But my dear Sir, my dear Sir, look – [*disdainful gesture, disgustedly*] – at the world – [*pause*] – and look – [*loving gesture, proudly*] – at my TROUSERS!'

[*Pause. He looks at* NELL *who has remained impassive, her eyes unseeing, breaks into a high forced laugh, cuts it short, pokes his head towards* NELL, *launches his laugh again.*]

HAMM: Silence!

[NAGG *starts, cuts short his laugh.*]

NELL: You could see down to the bottom.

HAMM: [*Exasperated.*] Have you not finished? Will you never finish? [*With sudden fury.*] Will this never finish? [NAGG *disappears into his bin, closes the lid behind him.* NELL *does not move. Frenziedly.*] My kingdom for a nightman! [*He whistles. Enter* CLOV.] Clear away this muck! Chuck it in the sea! [CLOV *goes to bins, halts.*]

NELL: So white.

HAMM: What? What's she blathering about?

[CLOV *stoops, takes* NELL*'s hand, feels her pulse.*]

NELL: [*To* CLOV.] Desert!

[CLOV *lets go her hand, pushes her back in the bin, closes the lid.*]

CLOV: [*Returning to his place beside the chair.*] She has no pulse.

HAMM: What was she drivelling about?

CLOV: She told me to go away, into the desert.

HAMM: Damn busybody! Is that all?

CLOV: No.

HAMM: What else?

CLOV: I didn't understand.

HAMM: Have you bottled her?

CLOV: Yes.

HAMM: Are they both bottled?

CLOV: Yes.

HAMM: Screw down the lids. [CLOV *goes towards door.*] Time enough. [CLOV *halts.*] My anger subsides, I'd like to pee.

CLOV: [*With alacrity.*] I'll go and get the catheter.

[*He goes towards the door.*]

HAMM: Time enough. [CLOV *halts.*] Give me my pain-killer.

CLOV: It's too soon. [*Pause.*] It's too soon on top of your tonic, it wouldn't act.

HAMM: In the morning they brace you up and in the evening they calm you down. Unless it's the other way round. [*Pause.*] That old doctor, he's dead, naturally?

CLOV: He wasn't old.

HAMM: But he's dead?

CLOV: Naturally. [*Pause.*] *You* ask *me* that?
[*Pause.*]

HAMM: Take me for a little turn. [CLOV *goes behind the chair and pushes it forward.*] Not too fast! [CLOV *pushes chair.*] Right round the world! [CLOV *pushes chair.*] Hug the walls, then back to the centre again. [CLOV *pushes chair.*] I was right in the centre, wasn't I?

CLOV: [*Pushing.*] Yes.

HAMM: We'd need a proper wheel-chair. With big wheels. Bicycle wheels! [*Pause.*] Are you hugging?

CLOV: [*Pushing.*] Yes.

HAMM: [*Groping for wall.*] It's a lie! Why do you lie to me?

CLOV: [*Bearing closer to wall.*] There! There!

HAMM: Stop! [CLOV *stops chair close to back wall.* HAMM *lays his hand against wall.*] Old wall! [*Pause.*] Beyond is the . . . other hell. [*Pause. Violently.*] Closer! Closer! Up against!

CLOV: Take away your hand. [HAMM *withdraws his hand.* CLOV *rams chair against wall.*] There!
[HAMM *leans towards wall, applies his ear to it.*]

HAMM: Do you hear? [*He strikes the wall with his knuckles.*] Do you hear? Hollow bricks! [*He strikes again.*] All that's hollow! [*Pause. He straightens up. Violently.*] That's enough. Back!

CLOV: We haven't done the round.

HAMM: Back to my place! [CLOV *pushes chair back to centre.*] Is that my place?

CLOV: Yes, that's your place.

HAMM: Am I right in the centre?

CLOV: I'll measure it.

HAMM: More or less! More or less!

CLOV: [*Moving chair slightly.*] There!

HAMM: I'm more or less in the centre?

CLOV: I'd say so.

HAMM: You'd say so! Put me right in the centre!

CLOV: I'll go and get the tape.

HAMM: Roughly! Roughly! [CLOV *moves chair slightly.*] Bang in the centre!

CLOV: There!

[*Pause.*]

HAMM: I feel a little too far to the left. [CLOV *moves chair slightly.*] Now I feel a little too far to the right. [CLOV *moves chair slightly.*] I feel a little too far forward. [CLOV *moves chair slightly.*] Now I feel a little too far back. [CLOV *moves chair slightly.*] Don't stay there [*i.e. behind the chair*], you give me the shivers.

[CLOV *returns to his place beside the chair.*]

CLOV: If I could kill him I'd die happy.

[*Pause.*]

HAMM: What's the weather like?

CLOV: The same as usual.

HAMM: Look at the earth.

CLOV: I've looked.

HAMM: With the glass?

CLOV: No need of the glass.

HAMM: Look at it with the glass.

CLOV: I'll go and get the glass.

[*Exit* CLOV.]

HAMM: No need of the glass!

[*Enter* CLOV *with telescope.*]

CLOV: I'm back again, with the glass. [*He goes to window right, looks up at it.*] I need the steps.

HAMM: Why? Have you shrunk? [*Exit* CLOV *with telescope.*] I don't like that, I don't like that.

[*Enter* CLOV *with ladder, but without telescope.*]

CLOV: I'm back again, with the steps. [*He sets down ladder under window right, gets up on it, realizes he has not the telescope, gets down.*] I need the glass.

[*He goes towards the door.*]

HAMM: [*Violently.*] But you have the glass!

CLOV: [*Halting, violently.*] No I haven't the glass!
[*Exit* CLOV.]

HAMM: This is deadly.
[*Enter* CLOV *with telescope. He goes towards ladder.*]

CLOV: Things are livening up. [*He gets up on ladder, raises the telescope, lets it fall.*] I did it on purpose. [*He gets down, picks up the telescope, turns it on auditorium.*] I see . . . a multitude . . . in transports . . . of joy. [*Pause.*] That's what I call a magnifier. [*He lowers the telescope, turns towards* HAMM.] Well? Don't we laugh?

HAMM: [*After reflection.*] I don't.

CLOV: [*After reflection.*] Nor I. [*He gets up on ladder, turns the telescope on the without.*] Let's see. [*He looks, moving the telescope.*] Zero . . . [*he looks*] . . . zero . . . [*he looks*] . . . and zero.

HAMM: Nothing stirs. All is—

CLOV: Zer—

HAMM: [*Violently.*] Wait till you're spoken to! [*Normal voice.*] All is . . . all is . . . all is what? [*Violently.*] All is what?

CLOV: What all is? In a word? Is that what you want to know? Just a moment. [*He turns the telescope on the without, looks, lowers the telescope, turns towards* HAMM.] Corpsed. [*Pause.*] Well? Content?

HAMM: Look at the sea.

CLOV: It's the same.

HAMM: Look at the ocean!
[CLOV *gets down, takes a few steps towards window left, goes back for ladder, carries it over and sets it down under window left, gets up on it, turns the telescope on the without, looks at length. He starts, lowers the telescope, examines it, turns it again on the without.*]

CLOV: Never seen anything like that!

HAMM: [*Anxious.*] What? A sail? A fin? Smoke?

CLOV: [*Looking.*] The light is sunk.

HAMM: [*Relieved.*] Pah! We all knew that.

CLOV: [*Looking.*] There was a bit left.

HAMM: The base.

CLOV: [*Looking.*] Yes.

HAMM: And now?

CLOV: [*Looking.*] All gone.

HAMM: No gulls?

CLOV: [*Looking.*] Gulls!

HAMM: And the horizon? Nothing on the horizon?

CLOV: [*Lowering the telescope, turning towards* HAMM, *exasperated.*] What in God's name could there be on the horizon?

[*Pause.*]

HAMM: The waves, how are the waves?

CLOV: The waves? [*He turns the telescope on the waves.*] Lead.

HAMM: And the sun?

CLOV: [*Looking.*] Zero.

HAMM: But it should be sinking. Look again.

CLOV: [*Looking.*] Damn the sun.

HAMM: Is it night already then?

CLOV: [*Looking.*] No.

HAMM: Then what is it?

CLOV: [*Looking.*] Grey. [*Lowering the telescope, turning towards* HAMM, *louder.*] Grey! [*Pause. Still louder.*] GRREY!
[*Pause. He gets down, approaches* HAMM *from behind, whispers in his ear.*]

HAMM: [*Starting.*] Grey! Did I hear you say grey?

CLOV: Light black. From pole to pole.

HAMM: You exaggerate. [*Pause.*] Don't stay there, you give me the shivers.

[CLOV *returns to his place beside the chair.*]

CLOV: Why this farce, day after day?

HAMM: Routine. One never knows. [*Pause.*] Last night I saw inside my breast. There was a big sore.

CLOV: Pah! You saw your heart.

HAMM: No, it was living. [*Pause. Anguished.*] Clov!

CLOV: Yes.

HAMM: What's happening?

CLOV: Something is taking its course.
[*Pause.*]
HAMM: Clov!
CLOV: [*Impatiently.*] What is it?
HAMM: We're not beginning to . . . to . . . mean something?
CLOV: Mean something! You and I, mean something! [*Brief laugh.*] Ah that's a good one!
HAMM: I wonder. [*Pause.*] Imagine if a rational being came back to earth, wouldn't he be liable to get ideas into his head if he observed us long enough. [*Voice of rational being.*] Ah, good, now I see what it is, yes, now I understand what they're at! [CLOV *starts, drops the telescope and begins to scratch his belly with both hands. Normal voice.*] And without going so far as that, we ourselves . . . [*with emotion*] . . . we ourselves . . . at certain moments . . . [*Vehemently.*] To think perhaps it won't all have been for nothing!
CLOV: [*Anguished, scratching himself.*] I have a flea!
HAMM: A flea! Are there still fleas?
CLOV: On me there's one. [*Scratching.*] Unless it's a crablouse.
HAMM: [*Very perturbed.*] But humanity might start from there all over again! Catch him, for the love of God!
CLOV: I'll go and get the powder.
[*Exit* CLOV.]
HAMM: A flea! This is awful! What a day!
[*Enter* CLOV *with a sprinkling-tin.*]
CLOV: I'm back again, with the insecticide.
HAMM: Let him have it!
[CLOV *loosens the top of his trousers, pulls it forward and shakes powder into the aperture. He stoops, looks, waits, starts, frenziedly shakes more powder, stoops, looks, waits.*]
CLOV: The bastard!
HAMM: Did you get him?
CLOV: Looks like it. [*He drops the tin and adjusts his trousers.*] Unless he's laying doggo.
HAMM: Laying! Lying you mean. Unless he's *lying* doggo.

CLOV: Ah? One says lying? One doesn't say laying?

HAMM: Use your head, can't you. If he was laying we'd be bitched.

CLOV: Ah. [*Pause.*] What about that pee?

HAMM: I'm having it.

CLOV: Ah that's the spirit, that's the spirit!
[*Pause.*]

HAMM: [*With ardour.*] Let's go from here, the two of us! South! You can make a raft and the currents will carry us away, far away, to other . . . mammals!

CLOV: God forbid!

HAMM: Alone, I'll embark alone! Get working on that raft immediately. Tomorrow I'll be gone for ever.

CLOV: [*Hastening towards door.*] I'll start straight away.

HAMM: Wait! [CLOV *halts.*] Will there be sharks, do you think?

CLOV: Sharks? I don't know. If there are there will be.
[*He goes towards door.*]

HAMM: Wait! [CLOV *halts.*] Is it not yet time for my pain-killer?

CLOV: [*Violently.*] No!
[*He goes towards door.*]

HAMM: Wait! [CLOV *halts.*] How are your eyes?

CLOV: Bad.

HAMM: But you can see.

CLOV: All I want.

HAMM: How are your legs?

CLOV: Bad.

HAMM: But you can walk.

CLOV: I come . . . and go.

HAMM: In my house. [*Pause. With prophetic relish.*] One day you'll be blind, like me. You'll be sitting there, a speck in the void, in the dark, for ever, like me. [*Pause.*] One day you'll say to yourself, I'm tired, I'll sit down, and you'll go and sit down. Then you'll say, I'm hungry, I'll get up and get something to eat. But you won't get up. You'll say, I shouldn't have sat down, but since I have I'll sit on a little longer, then I'll get up and get something to eat.

But you won't get up and you won't get anything to eat. [*Pause.*] You'll look at the wall a while, then you'll say, I'll close my eyes, perhaps have a little sleep, after that I'll feel better, and you'll close them. And when you open them again there'll be no wall any more. [*Pause.*] Infinite emptiness will be all around you, all the resurrected dead of all the ages wouldn't fill it, and there you'll be like a little bit of grit in the middle of the steppe. [*Pause.*] Yes, one day you'll know what it is, you'll be like me, except that you won't have anyone with you, because you won't have had pity on anyone and because there won't be anyone left to have pity on.
[*Pause.*]

CLOV: It's not certain. [*Pause.*] And there's one thing you forget.

HAMM: Ah?

CLOV: I can't sit down.

HAMM: [*Impatiently.*] Well, you'll lie down then, what the hell! Or you'll come to a standstill, simply stop and stand still, the way you are now. One day you'll say, I'm tired, I'll stop. What does the attitude matter?
[*Pause.*]

CLOV: So you all want me to leave you.

HAMM: Naturally.

CLOV: Then I'll leave you.

HAMM: You can't leave us.

CLOV: Then I shan't leave you.
[*Pause.*]

HAMM: Why don't you finish us? [*Pause.*] I'll tell you the combination of the larder if you promise to finish me.

CLOV: I couldn't finish you.

HAMM: Then you shan't finish me.
[*Pause.*]

CLOV: I'll leave you, I have things to do.

HAMM: Do you remember when you came here?

CLOV: No. Too small, you told me.

HAMM: Do you remember your father?

CLOV: [*Wearily.*] Same answer. [*Pause.*] You've asked me these questions millions of times.

HAMM: I love the old questions. [*With fervour.*] Ah the old questions, the old answers, there's nothing like them! [*Pause.*] It was I was a father to you.

CLOV: Yes. [*He looks at* HAMM *fixedly.*] You were that to me.

HAMM: My house a home for you.

CLOV: Yes. [*He looks about him.*] This was that for me.

HAMM: [*Proudly.*] But for me [*gesture towards himself*] no father. But for Hamm [*gesture towards surroundings*] no home.
[*Pause.*]

CLOV: I'll leave you.

HAMM: Did you ever think of one thing?

CLOV: Never.

HAMM: That here we're down in a hole. [*Pause.*] But beyond the hills? Eh? Perhaps it's still green. Eh? [*Pause.*] Flora! Pomona! [*Ecstatically.*] Ceres! [*Pause.*] Perhaps you won't need to go very far.

CLOV: I can't go very far. [*Pause.*] I'll leave you.

HAMM: Is my dog ready?

CLOV: He lacks a leg.

HAMM: Is he silky?

CLOV: He's a kind of Pomeranian.

HAMM: Go and get him.

CLOV: He lacks a leg.

HAMM: Go and get him! [*Exit* CLOV.] We're getting on.
[*Enter* CLOV *holding by one of its three legs a black toy dog.*]

CLOV: Your dogs are here.
[*He hands the dog to* HAMM *who feels it, fondles it.*]

HAMM: He's white, isn't he?

CLOV: Nearly.

HAMM: What do you mean, nearly? Is he white or isn't he?

CLOV: He isn't.
[*Pause.*]

HAMM: You've forgotten the sex.

CLOV: [*Vexed.*] But he isn't finished. The sex goes on at the end.

[*Pause.*]

HAMM: You haven't put on his ribbon.

CLOV: [*Angrily.*] But he isn't finished, I tell you! First you finish your dog and then you put on his ribbon!

[*Pause.*]

HAMM: Can he stand?

CLOV: I don't know.

HAMM: Try. [*He hands the dog to* CLOV *who places it on the ground.*] Well?

CLOV: Wait!

[*He squats down and tries to get the dog to stand on its three legs, fails, lets it go. The dog falls on its side.*]

HAMM: [*Impatiently.*] Well?

CLOV: He's standing.

HAMM: [*Groping for the dog.*] Where? Where is he?

[CLOV *holds up the dog in a standing position.*]

CLOV: There.

[*He takes* HAMM'*s hand and guides it towards the dog's head.*]

HAMM: [*His hand on the dog's head.*] Is he gazing at me?

CLOV: Yes.

HAMM: [*Proudly.*] As if he were asking me to take him for a walk?

CLOV: If you like.

HAMM: [*As before.*] Or as if he were begging me for a bone. [*He withdraws his hand.*] Leave him like that, standing there imploring me.

[CLOV *straightens up. The dog falls on its side.*]

CLOV: I'll leave you.

HAMM: Have you had your visions?

CLOV: Less.

HAMM: Is Mother Pegg's light on?

CLOV: Light! How could anyone's light be on?

HAMM: Extinguished!

CLOV: Naturally it's extinguished. If it's not on it's extinguished.

HAMM: No, I mean Mother Pegg.

CLOV: But naturally she's extinguished! [*Pause.*] What's the matter with you today?

HAMM: I'm taking my course. [*Pause.*] Is she buried?

CLOV: Buried! Who would have buried her?

HAMM: You.

CLOV: Me! Haven't I enough to do without burying people?

HAMM: But you'll bury me.

CLOV: No I shan't bury you.

[*Pause.*]

HAMM: She was bonny once, like a flower of the field. [*With reminiscent leer.*] And a great one for the men!

CLOV: We too were bonny – once. It's a rare thing not to have been bonny – once.

[*Pause.*]

HAMM: Go and get the gaff.

[CLOV *goes to door, halts.*]

CLOV: Do this, do that, and I do it. I never refuse. Why?

HAMM: You're not able to.

CLOV: Soon I won't do it any more.

HAMM: You won't be able to any more. [*Exit* CLOV.] Ah the creatures, the creatures, everything has to be explained to them.

[*Enter* CLOV *with gaff.*]

CLOV: Here's your gaff. Stick it up.

[*He gives the gaff to* HAMM *who, wielding it like a puntpole, tries to move his chair.*]

HAMM: Did I move?

CLOV: No.

[HAMM *throws down the gaff.*]

HAMM: Go and get the oilcan.

CLOV: What for?

HAMM: To oil the castors.

27

CLOV: I oiled them yesterday.

HAMM: Yesterday! What does that mean? Yesterday!

CLOV: [*Violently.*] That means that bloody awful day, long ago, before this bloody awful day. I use the words you taught me. If they don't mean anything any more, teach me others. Or let me be silent.

[*Pause.*]

HAMM: I once knew a madman who thought the end of the world had come. He was a painter – and engraver. I had a great fondness for him. I used to go and see him, in the asylum. I'd take him by the hand and drag him to the window. Look! There! All that rising corn! And there! Look! The sails of the herring fleet! All that loveliness! [*Pause.*] He'd snatch away his hand and go back into his corner. Appalled. All he had seen was ashes. [*Pause.*] He alone had been spared. [*Pause.*] Forgotten. [*Pause.*] It appears the case is . . . was not so . . . so unusual.

CLOV: A madman? When was that?

HAMM: Oh way back, way back, you weren't in the land of the living.

CLOV: God be with the days!

[*Pause.* HAMM *raises his toque.*]

HAMM: I had a great fondness for him. [*Pause. He puts on his toque again.*] He was a painter – and engraver.

CLOV: There are so many terrible things.

HAMM: No, no, there are not so many now. [*Pause.*] Clov!

CLOV: Yes.

HAMM: Do you not think this has gone on long enough?

CLOV: Yes! [*Pause.*] What?

HAMM: This . . . this . . . thing.

CLOV: I've always thought so. [*Pause.*] You not?

HAMM: [*Gloomily.*] Then it's a day like any other day.

CLOV: As long as it lasts. [*Pause.*] All life long the same inanities.

[*Pause.*]

HAMM: I can't leave you.

CLOV: I know. And you can't follow me.
   [*Pause.*]

HAMM: If you leave me how shall I know?

CLOV: [*Briskly.*] Well you simply whistle me and if I don't
   come running it means I've left you.
   [*Pause.*]

HAMM: You won't come and kiss me good-bye?

CLOV: Oh I shouldn't think so.
   [*Pause.*]

HAMM: But you might be merely dead in your kitchen.

CLOV: The result would be the same.

HAMM: Yes, but how would I know, if you were merely dead
   in your kitchen?

CLOV: Well . . . sooner or later I'd start to stink.

HAMM: You stink already. The whole place stinks of corpses.

CLOV: The whole universe.

HAMM: [*Angrily.*] To hell with the universe! [*Pause.*] Think of
   something.

CLOV: What?

HAMM: An idea, have an idea. [*Angrily.*] A bright idea!

CLOV: Ah good. [*He starts pacing to and fro, his eyes fixed on
   the ground, his hands behind his back. He halts.*] The pains
   in my legs! It's unbelievable! Soon I won't be able to
   think any more.

HAMM: You won't be able to leave me. [CLOV *resumes his
   pacing.*] What are you doing?

CLOV: Having an idea. [*He paces.*] Ah!
   [*He halts.*]

HAMM: What a brain! [*Pause.*] Well?

CLOV: Wait! [*He meditates. Not very convinced.*] Yes . . . [*Pause.
   More convinced.*] Yes! [*He raises his head.*] I have it! I set
   the alarm.
   [*Pause.*]

HAMM: This is perhaps not one of my bright days, but
   frankly—

CLOV: You whistle me. I don't come. The alarm rings. I'm gone. It doesn't ring. I'm dead.
[*Pause.*]

HAMM: Is it working? [*Pause. Impatiently.*] The alarm, is it working?

CLOV: Why wouldn't it be working?

HAMM: Because it's worked too much.

CLOV: But it's hardly worked at all.

HAMM: [*Angrily.*] Then because it's worked too little!

CLOV: I'll go and see. [*Exit* CLOV. *Brief ring of alarm off. Enter* CLOV *with alarm-clock. He holds it against* HAMM's *ear and releases alarm. They listen to it ringing to the end. Pause.*] Fit to wake the dead! Did you hear it?

HAMM: Vaguely.

CLOV: The end is terrific!

HAMM: I prefer the middle. [*Pause.*] Is it not time for my pain-killer?

CLOV: No! [*He goes to the door, turns.*] I'll leave you.

HAMM: It's time for my story. Do you want to listen to my story?

CLOV: No.

HAMM: Ask my father if he wants to listen to my story.
[CLOV *goes to bins, raises the lid of* NAGG's, *stoops, looks into it. Pause. He straightens up.*]

CLOV: He's asleep.

HAMM: Wake him.
[CLOV *stoops, wakes* NAGG *with the alarm. Unintelligible words.* CLOV *straightens up.*]

CLOV: He doesn't want to listen to your story.

HAMM: I'll give him a bon-bon.
[CLOV *stoops. As before.*]

CLOV: He wants a sugar-plum.

HAMM: He'll get a sugar-plum.
[CLOV *stoops. As before.*]

CLOV: It's a deal. [*He goes towards door.* NAGG's *hands appear, gripping the rim. Then the head emerges.* CLOV *reaches door, turns.*] Do you believe in the life to come?

HAMM: Mine was always that. [*Exit* CLOV.] Got him that time!

NAGG: I'm listening.

HAMM: Scoundrel! Why did you engender me?

NAGG: I didn't know.

HAMM: What? What didn't you know?

NAGG: That it'd be you. [*Pause.*] You'll give me a sugar-plum?

HAMM: After the audition.

NAGG: You swear?

HAMM: Yes.

NAGG: On what?

HAMM: My honour.

[*Pause. They laugh heartily.*]

NAGG: Two.

HAMM: One.

NAGG: One for me and one for—

HAMM: One! Silence! [*Pause.*] Where was I? [*Pause. Gloomily.*] It's finished, we're finished. [*Pause.*] Nearly finished. [*Pause.*] There'll be no more speech. [*Pause.*] Something dripping in my head, ever since the fontanelles. [*Stifled hilarity of* NAGG.] Splash, splash, always on the same spot. [*Pause.*] Perhaps it's a little vein. [*Pause.*] A little artery. [*Pause. More animated.*] Enough of that, it's story time, where was I? [*Pause. Narrative tone.*] The man came crawling towards me, on his belly. Pale, wonderfully pale and thin, he seemed on the point of – [*Pause. Normal tone.*] No, I've done that bit. [*Pause. Narrative tone.*] I calmly filled my pipe – the meerschaum, lit it with . . . let us say a vesta, drew a few puffs. Aah! [*Pause.*] Well, what is it *you* want? [*Pause.*] It was an extra-ordinarily bitter day, I remember, zero by the thermometer. But considering it was Christmas Eve there was nothing . . . extra-ordinary about that. Seasonable weather, for once in a way. [*Pause.*] Well, what ill wind blows you my way? He raised his face to me, black with mingled dirt and tears. [*Pause. Normal tone.*] That should do it. [*Narrative*

tone.] No, no, don't look at me, don't look at me. He
dropped his eyes and mumbled something, apologies
I presume. [*Pause*.] I'm a busy man, you know, the final
touches, before the festivities, you know what it is.
[*Pause. Forcibly*.] Come on now, what is the object of this
invasion? [*Pause*.] It was a glorious bright day, I
remember, fifty by the heliometer, but already the sun
was sinking down into the . . . down among the dead.
[*Normal tone*.] Nicely put, that. [*Narrative tone*.] Come
on now, come on, present your petition and let me
resume my labours. [*Pause. Normal tone*.] There's
English for you. Ah well . . . [*Narrative tone*.] It was then
he took the plunge. It's my little one, he said. Tsstss, a
little one, that's bad. My little boy, he said, as if the sex
mattered. Where did he come from? He named the hole.
A good half-day, on horse. What are you insinuating?
That the place is still inhabited? No no, not a soul,
except himself and the child – assuming he existed.
Good. I inquired about the situation at Kov, beyond the
gulf. Not a sinner. Good. And you expect me to believe
you have left your little one back there, all alone, and
alive into the bargain? Come now! [*Pause*.] It was a
howling wild day, I remember, a hundred by the
anemometer. The wind was tearing up the dead pines
and sweeping them . . . away. [*Pause. Normal tone*.] A bit
feeble, that. [*Narrative tone*.] Come on, man, speak up,
what is it you want from me, I have to put up my holly.
[*Pause*.] Well to make it short it finally transpired that
what he wanted from me was . . . bread for his brat.
Bread? But I have no bread, it doesn't agree with me.
Good. Then perhaps a little corn? [*Pause. Normal tone*.]
That should do it. [*Narrative tone*.] Corn, yes, I have
corn, it's true, in my granaries. But use your head. I give
you some corn, a pound, a pound and a half, you bring it
back to your child and you make him – if he's still alive –
a nice pot of porridge [NAGG *reacts*], a nice pot and a

half of porridge, full of nourishment. Good. The colours come back into his little cheeks – perhaps. And then? [*Pause.*] I lost patience. [*Violently.*] Use your head, can't you, use your head, you're on earth, there's no cure for that! [*Pause.*] It was an exceedingly dry day, I remember, zero by the hygrometer. Ideal weather, for my lumbago. [*Pause. Violently.*] But what in God's name do you imagine? That the earth will awake in spring? That the rivers and seas will run with fish again? That there's manna in heaven still for imbeciles like you? [*Pause.*] Gradually I cooled down, sufficiently at least to ask him how long he had taken on the way. Three whole days. Good. In what condition he had left the child. Deep in sleep. [*Forcibly.*] But deep in what sleep, deep in what sleep already? [*Pause.*] Well to make it short I finally offered to take him into my service. He had touched a chord. And then I imagined already that I wasn't much longer for this world. [*He laughs. Pause.*] Well? [*Pause.*] Well? Here if you were careful you might die a nice natural death, in peace and comfort. [*Pause.*] Well? [*Pause.*] In the end he asked me would I consent to take in the child as well – if he were still alive. [*Pause.*] It was the moment I was waiting for. [*Pause.*] Would I consent to take in the child . . . [*Pause.*] I can see him still, down on his knees, his hands flat on the ground, glaring at me with his mad eyes, in defiance of my wishes. [*Pause. Normal tone.*] I'll soon have finished with this story. [*Pause.*] Unless I bring in other characters. [*Pause.*] But where would I find them? [*Pause.*] Where would I look for them? [*Pause. He whistles. Enter* CLOV.] Let us pray to God.

NAGG: Me sugar-plum!

CLOV: There's a rat in the kitchen!

HAMM: A rat! Are there still rats?

CLOV: In the kitchen there's one.

HAMM: And you haven't exterminated him?

CLOV: Half. You disturbed us.

HAMM: He can't get away?

CLOV: No.

HAMM: You'll finish him later. Let us pray to God.

CLOV: Again!

NAGG: Me sugar-plum!

HAMM: God first! [*Pause.*] Are you right?

CLOV: [*Resigned.*] Off we go.

HAMM: [*To* NAGG.] And you?

NAGG: [*Clasping his hands, closing his eyes, in a gabble.*] Our Father which art—

HAMM: Silence! In silence! Where are your manners? [*Pause.*] Off we go. [*Attitudes of prayer. Silence. Abandoning his attitude, discouraged.*] Well?

CLOV: [*Abandoning his attitude.*] What a hope! And you?

HAMM: Sweet damn all! [*To* NAGG.] And you?

NAGG: Wait! [*Pause. Abandoning his attitude.*] Nothing doing!

HAMM: The bastard! He doesn't exist!

CLOV: Not yet.

NAGG: Me sugar-plum!

HAMM: There are no more sugar-plums!

[*Pause.*]

NAGG: It's natural. After all I'm your father. It's true if it hadn't been me it would have been someone else. But that's no excuse. [*Pause.*] Turkish Delight, for example, which no longer exists, we all know that, there is nothing in the world I love more. And one day I'll ask you for some, in return for a kindness, and you'll promise it to me. One must live with the times. [*Pause.*] Whom did you call when you were a tiny boy, and were frightened, in the dark? Your mother? No. Me. We let you cry. Then we moved you out of earshot, so that we might sleep in peace. [*Pause.*] I was asleep, as happy as a king, and you woke me up to have me listen to you. It wasn't indispensable, you didn't really need to have me listen to you. Besides I didn't listen to you. [*Pause.*] I hope the

day will come when you'll really need to have me listen
to you, and need to hear my voice, any voice. [*Pause.*]
Yes, I hope I'll live till then, to hear you calling me like
when you were a tiny boy, and were frightened, in the
dark, and I was your only hope. [*Pause.* NAGG *knocks on
lid of* NELL's *bin. Pause.*] Nell! [*Pause. He knocks louder.
Pause. Louder.*] Nell! [*Pause.* NAGG *sinks back into his bin,
closes the lid behind him. Pause.*]

HAMM: Our revels now are ended. [*He gropes for the dog.*]
The dog's gone.

CLOV: He's not a real dog, he can't go.

HAMM: [*Groping.*] He's not there.

CLOV: He's lain down.

HAMM: Give him up to me. [CLOV *picks up the dog and gives it
to* HAMM. HAMM *holds it in his arms. Pause.* HAMM *throws
away the dog.*] Dirty brute! [CLOV *begins to pick up the
objects lying on the ground.*] What are you doing?

CLOV: Putting things in order. [*He straightens up. Fervently.*]
I'm going to clear everything away!
[*He starts picking up again.*]

HAMM: Order!

CLOV: [*Straightening up.*] I love order. It's my dream. A world
where all would be silent and still and each thing in its
last place, under the last dust.
[*He starts picking up again.*]

HAMM: [*Exasperated.*] What in God's name do you think you
are doing?

CLOV: [*Straightening up.*] I'm doing my best to create a little
order.

HAMM: Drop it!
[CLOV *drops the objects he has picked up.*]

CLOV: After all, there or elsewhere.
[*He goes towards door.*]

HAMM: [*Irritably.*] What's wrong with your feet?

CLOV: My feet?

HAMM: Tramp! Tramp!

CLOV: I must have put on my boots.

HAMM: Your slippers were hurting you?

[*Pause.*]

CLOV: I'll leave you.

HAMM: No!

CLOV: What is there to keep me here?

HAMM: The dialogue. [*Pause.*] I've got on with my story. [*Pause.*] I've got on with it well. [*Pause. Irritably.*] Ask me where I've got to.

CLOV: Oh, by the way, your story?

HAMM: [*Surprised.*] What story?

CLOV: The one you've been telling yourself all your . . . days.

HAMM: Ah you mean my chronicle?

CLOV: That's the one.

[*Pause.*]

HAMM: [*Angrily.*] Keep going, can't you, keep going!

CLOV: You've got on with it, I hope.

HAMM: [*Modestly.*] Oh not very far, not very far. [*He sighs.*] There are days like that, one isn't inspired. [*Pause.*] Nothing you can do about it, just wait for it to come. [*Pause.*] No forcing, no forcing, it's fatal. [*Pause.*] I've got on with it a little all the same. [*Pause.*] Technique, you know. [*Pause. Irritably.*] I say I've got on with it a little all the same.

CLOV: [*Admiringly.*] Well I never! In spite of everything you were able to get on with it!

HAMM: [*Modestly.*] Oh not very far, you know, not very far, but nevertheless, better than nothing.

CLOV: Better than nothing! Is it possible?

HAMM: I'll tell you how it goes. He comes crawling on his belly–

CLOV: Who?

HAMM: What?

CLOV: Who do you mean, he?

HAMM: Who do I mean! Yet another.

CLOV: Ah him! I wasn't sure.

HAMM: Crawling on his belly, whining for bread for his brat. He's offered a job as gardener. Before – [CLOV *bursts out laughing.*] What is there so funny about that?

CLOV: A job as gardener!

HAMM: Is that what tickles you?

CLOV: It must be that.

HAMM: It wouldn't be the bread?

CLOV: Or the brat.

[*Pause.*]

HAMM: The whole thing is comical, I grant you that. What about having a good guffaw the two of us together?

CLOV: [*After reflection.*] I couldn't guffaw again today.

HAMM: [*After reflection.*] Nor I. [*Pause.*] I continue then. Before accepting with gratitude he asks if he may have his little boy with him.

CLOV: What age?

HAMM: Oh tiny.

CLOV: He would have climbed the trees.

HAMM: All the little odd jobs.

CLOV: And then he would have grown up.

HAMM: Very likely.

[*Pause.*]

CLOV: Keep going, can't you, keep going!

HAMM: That's all. I stopped there.

[*Pause.*]

CLOV: Do you see how it goes on.

HAMM: More or less.

CLOV: Will it not soon be the end?

HAMM: I'm afraid it will.

CLOV: Pah! You'll make up another.

HAMM: I don't know. [*Pause.*] I feel rather drained. [*Pause.*] The prolonged creative effort. [*Pause.*] If I could drag myself down to the sea! I'd make a pillow of sand for my head and the tide would come.

CLOV: There's no more tide.
[*Pause.*]
HAMM: Go and see is she dead.
[CLOV *goes to bins, raises the lid of* NELL'*s, stoops, looks into it. Pause.*]
CLOV: Looks like it.
[*He closes the lid, straightens up.* HAMM *raises his toque. Pause. He puts it on again.*]
HAMM: [*With his hand to his toque.*] And Nagg?
[CLOV *raises lid of* NAGG'*s bin, stoops, looks into it. Pause.*]
CLOV: Doesn't look like it.
[*He closes the lid, straightens up.*]
HAMM: [*Letting go his toque.*] What's he doing?
[CLOV *raises lid of* NAGG'*s bin, stoops, looks into it. Pause.*]
CLOV: He's crying.
[*He closes the lid, straightens up.*]
HAMM: Then he's living. [*Pause.*] Did you ever have an instant of happiness?
CLOV: Not to my knowledge.
[*Pause.*]
HAMM: Bring me under the window. [CLOV *goes towards chair.*] I want to feel the light on my face. [CLOV *pushes chair.*] Do you remember, in the beginning, when you took me for a turn? You used to hold the chair too high. At every step you nearly tipped me out. [*With senile quaver.*] Ah great fun, we had, the two of us, great fun! [*Gloomily.*] And then we got into the way of it. [CLOV *stops the chair under window right.*] There already? [*Pause. He tilts back his head.*] Is it light?
CLOV: It isn't dark.
HAMM: [*Angrily.*] I'm asking you is it light?
CLOV: Yes.
[*Pause.*]
HAMM: The curtain isn't closed?
CLOV: No.

HAMM: What window is it?

CLOV: The earth.

HAMM: I knew it! [*Angrily.*] But there's no light there! The other! [CLOV *pushes chair towards window left.*] The earth! [CLOV *stops the chair under window left.* HAMM *tilts back his head.*] That's what I call light! [*Pause.*] Feels like a ray of sunshine. [*Pause.*] No?

CLOV: No.

HAMM: It isn't a ray of sunshine I feel on my face?

CLOV: No.

[*Pause.*]

HAMM: Am I very white? [*Pause. Angrily.*] I'm asking you am I very white!

CLOV: Not more so than usual.

[*Pause.*]

HAMM: Open the window.

CLOV: What for?

HAMM: I want to hear the sea.

CLOV: You wouldn't hear it.

HAMM: Even if you opened the window?

CLOV: No.

HAMM: Then it's not worth while opening it?

CLOV: No.

HAMM: [*Violently.*] Then open it! [CLOV *gets up on the ladder, opens the window. Pause.*] Have you opened it?

CLOV: Yes.

[*Pause.*]

HAMM: You swear you've opened it?

CLOV: Yes.

[*Pause.*]

HAMM: Well . . .! [*Pause.*] It must be very calm. [*Pause. Violently.*] I'm asking you is it very calm?

CLOV: Yes.

HAMM: It's because there are no more navigators. [*Pause.*] You haven't much conversation all of a sudden. Do you not feel well?

CLOV: I'm cold.

HAMM: What month are we? [*Pause.*] Close the window, we're going back. [CLOV *closes the window, gets down, pushes the chair back to its place, remains standing behind it, head bowed.*] Don't stay there, you give me the shivers! [CLOV *returns to his place beside the chair.*] Father! [*Pause. Louder.*] Father! [*Pause.*] Go and see did he hear me.
[CLOV *goes to* NAGG's *bin, raises the lid, stoops. Unintelligible words.* CLOV *straightens up.*]

CLOV: Yes.

HAMM: Both times?
[CLOV *stoops. As before.*]

CLOV: Once only.

HAMM: The first time or the second?
[CLOV *stoops. As before.*]

CLOV: He doesn't know.

HAMM: It must have been the second.

CLOV: We'll never know.
[*He closes lid.*]

HAMM: Is he still crying?

CLOV: No.

HAMM: The dead go fast. [*Pause.*] What's he doing?

CLOV: Sucking his biscuit.

HAMM: Life goes on. [CLOV *returns to his place beside the chair.*] Give me a rug, I'm freezing.

CLOV: There are no more rugs.
[*Pause.*]

HAMM: Kiss me. [*Pause.*] Will you not kiss me?

CLOV: No.

HAMM: On the forehead.

CLOV: I won't kiss you anywhere.
[*Pause.*]

HAMM: [*Holding out his hand.*] Give me your hand at least. [*Pause.*] Will you not give me your hand?

CLOV: I won't touch you.
[*Pause.*]

HAMM: Give me the dog. [CLOV *looks round for the dog.*] No!

CLOV: Do you not want your dog?

HAMM: No.

CLOV: Then I'll leave you.

HAMM: [*Head bowed, absently.*] That's right.

[CLOV *goes to door, turns.*]

CLOV: If I don't kill that rat he'll die.

HAMM: [*As before.*] That's right. [*Exit* CLOV. *Pause.*] Me to
play. [*He takes out his handkerchief, unfolds it, holds it spread
out before him.*] We're getting on. [*Pause.*] You weep, and
weep, for nothing, so as not to laugh, and little by little
. . . you begin to grieve. [*He folds the handkerchief, puts it
back in his pocket, raises his head.*] All those I might have
helped. [*Pause.*] Helped! [*Pause.*] Saved. [*Pause.*] Saved!
[*Pause.*] The place was crawling with them! [*Pause.
Violently.*] Use your head, can't you, use your head,
you're on earth, there's no cure for that! [*Pause.*] Get out
of here and love one another! Lick your neighbour as
yourself! [*Pause. Calmer.*] When it wasn't bread they
wanted it was crumpets. [*Pause. Violently.*] Out of my
sight and back to your petting parties [*Pause.*] All that, all
that! [*Pause.*] Not even a real dog! [*Calmer.*] The end is in
the beginning and yet you go on. [*Pause.*] Perhaps I
could go on with my story, end it and begin another.
[*Pause.*] Perhaps I could throw myself out on the floor.
[*He pushes himself painfully off his seat, falls back again.*]
Dig my nails into the cracks and drag myself forward
with my fingers. [*Pause.*] It will be the end and there I'll
be, wondering what can have brought it on and
wondering what can have . . . [*he hesitates*] . . . why it was
so long coming. [*Pause.*] There I'll be, in the old refuge,
alone against the silence and . . . [*he hesitates*] . . . the
stillness. If I can hold my peace, and sit quiet, it will be
all over with sound, and motion, all over and done with.
[*Pause.*] I'll have called my father and I'll have called my
. . . [*he hesitates*] . . . my son. And even twice, or three

times, in case they shouldn't have heard me, the first time, or the second. [*Pause.*] I'll say to myself, He'll come back. [*Pause.*] And then? [*Pause.*] And then? [*Pause.*] He couldn't, he has gone too far. [*Pause.*] And then? [*Pause. Very agitated.*] All kinds of fantasies! That I'm being watched! A rat! Steps! Breath held and then . . . [*he breathes out.*] Then babble, babble, words, like the solitary child who turns himself into children, two, three, so as to be together, and whisper together, in the dark. [*Pause.*] Moment upon moment, pattering down, like the millet grains of . . . [*he hesitates*] . . . that old Greek, and all life long you wait for that to mount up to a life. [*Pause. He opens his mouth to continue, renounces.*] Ah let's get it over! [*He whistles. Enter* CLOV *with alarm-clock. He halts beside the chair.*] What? Neither gone nor dead?

CLOV: In spirit only.

HAMM: Which?

CLOV: Both.

HAMM: Gone from me you'd be dead.

CLOV: And *vice versa.*

HAMM: Outside of here it's death! [*Pause.*] And the rat?

CLOV: He's got away.

HAMM: He can't go far. [*Pause. Anxious.*] Eh?

CLOV: He doesn't need to go far.

[*Pause.*]

HAMM: Is it not time for my pain-killer?

CLOV: Yes.

HAMM: Ah! At last! Give it to me! Quick!

[*Pause.*]

CLOV: There's no more pain-killer.

[*Pause.*]

HAMM: [*Appalled.*] Good . . .! [*Pause.*] No more pain-killer!

CLOV: No more pain-killer. You'll never get any more pain-killer.

[*Pause.*]

HAMM: But the little round box. It was full!

CLOV: Yes. But now it's empty.

[*Pause.* CLOV *starts to move about the room. He is looking for a place to put down the alarm-clock.*]

HAMM: [*Soft.*] What'll I do? [*Pause. In a scream.*] What'll I do? [CLOV *sees the picture, takes it down, stands it on the floor with its face to wall, hangs up the alarm-clock in its place.*] What are you doing?

CLOV: Winding up.

HAMM: Look at the earth.

CLOV: Again!

HAMM: Since it's calling to you.

CLOV: Is your throat sore? [*Pause.*] Would you like a lozenge? [*Pause.*] No? [*Pause.*] Pity.

[CLOV *goes, humming, towards window right, halts before it, looks up at it.*]

HAMM: Don't sing.

CLOV: [*Turning towards* HAMM.] One hasn't the right to sing any more?

HAMM: No.

CLOV: Then how can it end?

HAMM: You want it to end?

CLOV: I want to sing.

HAMM: I can't prevent you.

[*Pause.* CLOV *turns towards window right.*]

CLOV: What did I do with that steps? [*He looks round for ladder.*] You didn't see that steps? [*He sees it.*] Ah, about time. [*He goes towards window left.*] Sometimes I wonder if I'm in my right mind. Then it passes over and I'm as lucid as before. [*He gets up on ladder, looks out of window.*] Christ, she's under water! [*He looks.*] How can that be? [*He pokes forward his head, his hand above his eyes.*] It hasn't rained. [*He wipes the pane, looks. Pause.*] Ah what a mug I am! I'm on the wrong side! [*He gets down, takes a few steps towards window right.*] Under water! [*He goes back for ladder.*] What a mug I am! [*He carries ladder towards window right.*] Sometimes I wonder if I'm in my right senses. Then it passes off and I'm as intelligent as ever. [*He sets down ladder under window right, gets up on it, looks out of window. He turns towards* HAMM.] Any particular sector you fancy? Or merely the whole thing?

HAMM: Whole thing.

CLOV: The general effect? Just a moment.

[*He looks out of window. Pause.*]

HAMM: Clov.

CLOV: [*Absorbed.*] Mmm.

HAMM: Do you know what it is?

CLOV: [*As before.*] Mmm.

HAMM: I was never there. [*Pause.*] Clov!

CLOV: [*Turning towards* HAMM, *exasperated.*] What is it?

HAMM: I was never there.

CLOV: Lucky for you.

[*He looks out of window.*]

HAMM: Absent, always. It all happened without me. I don't know what's happened. [*Pause.*] Do you know what's happened? [*Pause.*] Clov!

CLOV: [*Turning towards* HAMM, *exasperated.*] Do you want me to look at this muckheap, yes or no?

HAMM: Answer me first.

CLOV: What?

HAMM: Do you know what's happened?

CLOV: When? Where?

HAMM: [*Violently.*] When! What's happened! Use your head, can't you! What has happened?

CLOV: What for Christ's sake does it matter?

[*He looks out of window.*]

HAMM: I don't know.

[*Pause.* CLOV *turns towards* HAMM.]

CLOV: [*Harshly.*] When old Mother Pegg asked you for oil for her lamp and you told her to get out to hell, you knew what was happening then, no? [*Pause.*] You know what she died of, Mother Pegg? Of darkness.

HAMM: [*Feebly.*] I hadn't any.

CLOV: [*As before.*] Yes, you had.
    [*Pause.*]
HAMM: Have you the glass?
CLOV: No, it's clear enough as it is.
HAMM: Go and get it.
    [*Pause.* CLOV *casts up his eyes, brandishes his fists. He loses balance, clutches on to the ladder. He starts to get down, halts.*]
CLOV: There's one thing I'll never understand. [*He gets down.*] Why I always obey you. Can you explain that to me?
HAMM: No . . . Perhaps it's compassion. [*Pause.*] A kind of great compassion. [*Pause.*] Oh you won't find it easy, you won't find it easy.
    [*Pause.* CLOV *begins to move about the room in search of the telescope.*]
CLOV: I'm tired of our goings on, very tired. [*He searches.*] You're not sitting on it?
    [*He moves the chair, looks at the place where it stood, resumes his search.*]
HAMM: [*Anguished.*] Don't leave me there! [*Angrily* CLOV *restores the chair to its place.*] Am I right in the centre?
CLOV: You'd need a microscope to find this – [*He sees the telescope.*] Ah, about time.
    [*He picks up the telescope, gets up on the ladder, turns the telescope on the without.*]
HAMM: Give me the dog.
CLOV: [*Looking.*] Quiet!
HAMM: [*Angrily.*] Give me the dog!
    [CLOV *drops the telescope, clasps his hands to his head. Pause. He gets down precipitately, looks for the dog, sees it, picks it up, hastens towards* HAMM *and strikes him on the head violently with the dog.*]
CLOV: There's your dog for you!
    [*The dog falls to the ground. Pause.*]
HAMM: He hit me!
CLOV: You drive me mad, I'm mad!

HAMM: If you must hit me, hit me with the axe. [*Pause.*] Or
with the gaff, hit me with the gaff. Not with the dog.
With the gaff. Or with the axe.
[CLOV *picks up the dog and gives it to* HAMM *who takes it in
his arms.*]

CLOV: [*Imploringly.*] Let's stop playing!

HAMM: Never! [*Pause.*] Put me in my coffin.

CLOV: There are no more coffins.

HAMM: Then let it end! [CLOV *goes towards ladder.*] With a
bang! [CLOV *gets up on ladder, gets down again, looks for
telescope, sees it, picks it up, gets up ladder, raises telescope.*]
Of darkness! And me? Did anyone ever have pity on me?

CLOV: [*Lowering the telescope, turning towards* HAMM.]
What? [*Pause.*] Is it me you're referring to?

HAMM: [*Angrily.*] An aside, ape! Did you never hear an
aside before? [*Pause.*] I'm warming up for my last
soliloquy.

CLOV: I warn you. I'm going to look at this filth since it's an
order. But it's the last time. [*He turns the telescope on the
without.*] Let's see. [*He moves the telescope.*] Nothing . . .
nothing . . . good . . . good . . . nothing . . . goo–
[*He starts, lowers the telescope, examines it, turns it again on
the without. Pause.*] Bad luck to it!

HAMM: More complications! [CLOV *gets down.*] Not an
underplot, I trust.
[CLOV *moves ladder nearer window, gets up on it, turns
telescope on the without.*]

CLOV: [*Dismayed.*] Looks like a small boy!

HAMM: [*Sarcastic.*] A small . . . boy!

CLOV: I'll go and see. [*He gets down, drops the telescope, goes
towards door, turns.*] I'll take the gaff.
[*He looks for the gaff, sees it, picks it up, hastens towards
door.*]

HAMM: No!
[CLOV *halts.*]

CLOV: No? A potential procreator?

HAMM: If he exists he'll die there or he'll come here. And if he doesn't . . .

[*Pause.*]

CLOV: You don't believe me? You think I'm inventing?

[*Pause.*]

HAMM: It's the end, Clov, we've come to the end. I don't need you any more.

[*Pause.*]

CLOV: Lucky for you.

[*He goes towards door.*]

HAMM: Leave me the gaff.

[CLOV *gives him the gaff, goes towards door, halts, looks at alarm-clock, takes it down, looks round for a better place to put it, goes to bins, puts it on lid of* NAGG's *bin. Pause.*]

CLOV: I'll leave you.

[*He goes towards door.*]

HAMM: Before you go . . . [CLOV *halts near door*] . . . say something.

CLOV: There is nothing to say.

HAMM: A few words . . . to ponder . . . in my heart.

CLOV: Your heart!

HAMM: Yes. [*Pause. Forcibly.*] Yes! [*Pause.*] With the rest, in the end, the shadows, the murmurs, all the trouble, to end up with. [*Pause.*] Clov . . . He never spoke to me. Then, in the end, before he went, without my having asked him, he spoke to me. He said . . .

CLOV: [*Despairingly.*] Ah . . .!

HAMM: Something . . . from your heart.

CLOV: My heart!

HAMM: A few words . . . from your heart.

[*Pause.*]

CLOV: [*Fixed gaze, tonelessly, towards auditorium.*] They said to me, That's love, yes yes, not a doubt, now you see how—

HAMM: Articulate!

CLOV: [*As before.*] How easy it is. They said to me. That's friendship, yes yes, no question, you've found it. They

47

said to me, Here's the place, stop, raise your head and look at all that beauty. That order! They said to me, Come now, you're not a brute beast, think upon these things and you'll see how all becomes clear. And simple! They said to me, What skilled attention they get, all these dying of their wounds.

HAMM: Enough!

CLOV: [*As before.*] I say to myself – sometimes, Clov, you must learn to suffer better than that if you want them to weary of punishing you – one day. I say to myself – sometimes, Clov, you must be there better than that if you want them to let you go – one day. But I feel too old, and too far, to form new habits. Good, it'll never end, I'll never go. [*Pause.*] Then one day, suddenly, it ends, it changes, I don't understand, it dies, or it's me, I don't understand that either. I ask the words that remain – sleeping, waking, morning, evening. They have nothing to say. [*Pause.*] I open the door of the cell and go. I am so bowed I only see my feet, if I open my eyes, and between my legs a little trail of black dust. I say to myself that the earth is extinguished, though I never saw it lit. [*Pause.*] It's easy going. [*Pause.*] When I fall I'll weep for happiness.

[*Pause. He goes towards door.*]

HAMM: Clov! [CLOV *halts, without turning.*] Nothing. [CLOV *moves on.*] Clov!

[CLOV *halts, without turning.*]

CLOV: This is what we call making an exit.

HAMM: I'm obliged to you, Clov. For your services.

CLOV: [*Turning, sharply.*] Ah pardon, it's I am obliged to you.

HAMM: It's we are obliged to each other. [*Pause.* CLOV *goes towards door.*] One thing more. [CLOV *halts.*] A last favour. [*Exit* CLOV.] Cover me with the sheet. [*Long pause.*] No? Good. [*Pause.*] Me to play. [*Pause. Wearily.*] Old endgame lost of old, play and lose and have done with losing. [*Pause. More animated.*] Let me see. [*Pause.*]

Ah yes! [*He tries to move the chair, using the gaff as before.
Enter* CLOV, *dressed for the road. Panama hat, tweed coat,
raincoat over his arm, umbrella, bag. He halts by the door
and stands there, impassive and motionless, his eyes fixed
on* HAMM, *till the end.* HAMM *gives up.*] Good. [*Pause.*]
Discard. [*He throws away the gaff, makes to throw away the
dog, thinks better of it.*] Take it easy. [*Pause.*] And now?
[*Pause.*] Raise hat. [*He raises his toque.*] Peace to our . . .
arses. [*Pause.*] And put on again. [*He puts on his toque.*]
Deuce. [*Pause. He takes off his glasses.*] Wipe. [*He takes out
his handkerchief and, without unfolding it, wipes his glasses.*]
And put on again. [*He puts on his glasses, puts back the
handkerchief in his pocket.*] We're coming. A few more
squirms like that and I'll call. [*Pause.*] A little poetry.
[*Pause.*] You prayed – [*Pause. He corrects himself.*] You
CRIED for night; it comes – [*Pause. He corrects himself.*]
It FALLS: now cry in darkness. [*He repeats, chanting.*]
You cried for night; it falls: now cry in darkness. [*Pause.*]
Nicely put, that. [*Pause.*] And now? [*Pause.*] Moments for
nothing, now as always, time was never and time is over,
reckoning closed and story ended. [*Pause. Narrative tone.*]
If he could have his child with him . . . [*Pause.*] It was the
moment I was waiting for. [*Pause.*] You don't want to
abandon him? You want him to bloom while you are
withering? Be there to solace your last million last
moments? [*Pause.*] He doesn't realize, all he knows is
hunger, and cold, and death to crown it all. But you! You
ought to know what the earth is like, nowadays. Oh, I put
him before his responsibilities! [*Pause. Normal tone.*] Well,
there we are, there I am, that's enough. [*He raises the
whistle to his lips, hesitates, drops it. Pause.*] Yes, truly! [*He
whistles. Pause. Louder. Pause.*] Good. [*Pause.*] Father!
[*Pause. Louder.*] Father! [*Pause.*] Good. [*Pause.*] We're
coming. [*Pause.*] And to end up with? [*Pause.*] Discard.
[*He throws away the dog. He tears the whistle from his neck.*]
With my compliments. [*He throws whistle towards*

auditorium. Pause. He sniffs. Soft.] Clov! [*Long pause.*] No?
Good. [*He takes out the handkerchief.*] Since that's the way
we're playing it . . . [*he unfolds handkerchief*] . . . let's play
it that way . . . [*he unfolds*] . . . and speak no more about
it . . . [*he finishes unfolding*] . . . speak no more. [*He holds
the handkerchief spread out before him.*] Old stancher!
[*Pause.*] You . . . remain. [*Pause. He covers his face with
handkerchief, lowers his arms to armrests, remains
motionless.*]
[*Brief tableau.*]

CURTAIN